CONFRONTATION

The approaching crisis
between the United States
and South Africa

Martin C. Spring

Seal Beach, California

First United States printing
in 1978 by '76 Press
P.O. Box 2686, Seal Beach, Ca. 90742

Paperback   ISBN   0 89245 012 6

Typesetting by Hilda Myburgh, Media Consultants (Pty) Ltd

To my wife Liz, for everything she has been and is to me.

Author's Note

This book has been written primarily for my American friends, in the hope that it will alert them to the deteriorating relations between 2 countries and the disturbing implications for both. Because of this, I have used American idiom, spelling and punctuation, and all financial amounts have been given in U.S. dollars at the exchange rate ruling in August 1977 (R1 = US $1.15). South African readers, please bear with me in this and understand why the book has been written this way.

Contents

1.

The move toward confrontation

The United States, the world's leading superpower, is headed for confrontation with South Africa, the world's most unpopular country. This much is clear, notwithstanding the continuing argument within the U.S. Administration over precisely how, how fast, and to what degree of severity, America should turn the heat on South Africa.

Public statements by Administration officials reflect confusion —either over what action should be taken, or over how the policy should be presented publicly. President Jimmy Carter talks of a willingness "to use all the levers we can to bring an end to the apartheid system." But Secretary of State Cyrus Vance says that the U.S. will not "try to impose American solutions for African problems." Vice-President Walter ("Fritz") Mondale, who is nominally in overall charge of the United States' Africa policy, has called for "full participation" of Blacks in the government of South Africa, which he clarified as meaning one man, one vote.

But State Department spokesman Hodding Carter says that the U.S. has no intention of imposing on South Africa any plan of any kind for advancing Black political rights.

In private meetings with South African Foreign Minister Roelof

("Pik") Botha and senior South African officials, however, top men in the Administration have been more consistent, and harsher, in explaining Washington's tough new policy toward Pretoria. Minister Botha has admitted as much, saying: "The United States has now threatened us with a worsening of relations if we do not toe the line according to their norms and standards—norms and standards which they themselves do not apply equally to all nations in the world."

According to American sources, the most serious of the specific threats that have been made include:

- Pressure on Iran and other Middle East sources to cut off their oil supplies to the Republic, which has no petroleum deposits of its own.
- Refusal in future on the part of the Western powers to exercise their vetoes in the U.N. Security Council to protect South Africa, as they have in the past, against worldwide mandatory sanctions on trade and other economic relations.
- Renewed U.S. Treasury gold sales to drive down the international bullion price, and thus do severe damage to the Republic's economy, which still depends on gold exports to provide about one-third of foreign exchange earnings.
- Action against U.S. industrial, mining and banking enterprises to stop, or at least to discourage, the already-diminished flow of loan and risk capital to South Africa, with diplomatic pressure on Western European countries to apply similar constraints to their business interests.

Many other punitive measures are under discussion in Washington, and a number of these have been mentioned in talks with South African Government representatives. The "hit list" includes:

- Limitation or even exclusion of South African exports to the U.S., which according to American sources earned $925-million in 1976. Possibly this would be done (as Long Island University Professor Donald G. Baker has put it) "through a reinterpretation of the Tariff Act of 1930, broadening its concept of 'forced labor'—and prohibitions against trade with countries using forced labor—to include South Africa, because its African workers have no real alternatives in terms of employment."

- Confiscation of any Namibian products shipped to the U.S., which would be in keeping with U.N. General Assembly resolutions.
- Pressure on the International Monetary Fund to suspend South Africa's credit facilities, or at least to impose tougher conditions as the price of any additional loans (the Republic borrowed $427-million from the IMF in the 12 months to March 1977).
- Freezing of South Africa-owned assets within the U.S., in much the same way as Britain froze Rhodesian assets after UDI in 1965.
- Restriction of visits to South Africa by American nationals, particularly tourists, by requiring previous State Department permission, just as such visits to certain Communist countries have been controlled in the past.
- Tougher visa requirements for South African nationals wishing to visit the U.S. (Japan already refuses visas for educational and sporting visits; many Third World countries will only issue visas to South Africans who sign statements condemning apartheid.)
- Provision of assistance to Black revolutionaries working for the overthrow of the South African and Rhodesian governments, for instance medical and other non-military supplies for the guerilla forces (which would, however, release guerilla funds that could then be used to buy arms), greater economic assistance to the Black African countries that allow their territory to be used by these forces for their operational and training bases, and a heightened "educational" campaign among Southern African Blacks, with the emphasis on how Blacks "broke" White resistance in the civil rights campaign in the U.S. South.
- Extension of the existing embargo on sales of U.S. arms to the Republic to include civilian equipment which can be used for military purposes, such as aircraft, trucks and computers.
- Pressure directly and via U.N. resolutions on France, Israel and other countries which do not apply arms embargoes to South Africa, or apply them to a lesser degree than the U.S., to cease all forms of military collaboration with the Republic.
- Severance of remaining links with the South African intelli-

gence services.

- Cessation of remaining links with the Republic in the field of peaceful use of nuclear power, and pressure on other countries such as France and West Germany to follow suit.
- Refusal to enrich South Africa-sourced uranium oxide on behalf of customers such as Japan.
- A ban on U.S. Export-Import Bank guarantees on loans to finance U.S. trade with the Republic.
- Suspension of South African Airways' landing rights in the U.S.
- A campaign of intense public criticism of the Republic, at the U.N. and elsewhere.

It is difficult to judge just how serious the U.S. is about the threats that it has been making, directly and indirectly. Some of them have been made before, for instance by Dr Henry Kissinger in 1976 when he was trying to secure the cooperation of the South African Prime Minister, John Vorster, in pressuring Rhodesia's premier Ian Smith into accepting Black majority rule in his country.

Certainly the Carter Administration is more likely to apply such punitive measures than was the Ford Administration, which became more moderate in its attitude towards South Africa as a working relationship evolved between Secretary of State Kissinger and Prime Minister Vorster. Vice-President Mondale told a leading South African Black newspaperman in May 1977 that President Carter would be giving a high priority to "smashing" apartheid during his first four-year term. This could be dismissed as the rhetoric of a politician telling someone what he wanted to hear, but it is consistent with the emergence of a more active, interventionist and critical policy towards South Africa which is causing a rapid and serious deterioration of relations between the U.S. and the Republic.

It is also consistent with the judgement of some perceptive Washington-watchers, and with Press reports. For instance the Washington columnist Henry Brandon has reported that President Carter "has taken on personal responsibility for African policy." John Barratt, Director of the South African Institute of International Affairs, said after meetings with influential members of the Administration in May 1977: "There is no doubt that President Carter has a greater personal interest in the problems of Southern Africa than any other American President, and this in itself means that the American approach to the issues of this region must be taken extremely seriously." It is suggested in Washington that it is common for an American President to try to "make his mark" in a particular region of foreign policy, with varying success (Kennedy in Latin America, Johnson in Vietnam, Nixon in China)—and that Carter has identified Southern Africa as his target area.

President Carter may or may not be deliberately seeking a confrontation with the South African Government. Officials tend to deny such an intention. But a confrontation there is going to be, whatever the intention, if the Administration carries through on almost any of the threats it has been making. And in fact the Administration's moral outlook, its view of the world, and political opportunism, all suggest an element of deliberate intent in seeking to provoke a public clash with South Africa.

Carter and the bright young men of his "Georgian Mafia", as is well known, relate the Southern African situation to their own race relations experiences in the U.S. South where various forms of pressure, and in particular economic pressure, produced dramatic change in the social, political and economic conditions experienced by Blacks. As one top policymaker told South African representatives in June 1977: "We're like reformed alcoholics. We've given up racism, and we're determined to get you off the bottle ... fast."

There are enormous differences between the situations in the American and African souths. The most obvious is that White Southerners never felt that their basic freedoms would be threatened by allowing Blacks their rights. It would not mean Black rule in Washington DC, or even in Montgomery, Alabama. South African Whites know that majority rule would mean Black rule, and they fear that this would lead to the destruction of their fundamental freedoms and their whole way of life. "The feeling of insecurity is heightened by a hostile Black continent, as well as by the violence and disorder in neighboring states," says John Barratt. Another difference is that Blacks and Whites in the U.S. South speak the same language, and share in so many respects the same political and cultural heritage (even civil rights were fought in terms of a Constitution written by the White Founding Fathers). Blacks and Whites in South Africa have little in common other than living in the same country and participating in a common economy. The whole thrust of American development, from earliest times, has been toward an integrated society, whereas the races in South Africa have

15

always lived apart. A third difference is that Black movements in the U.S. South sought civil rights using political and economic pressure through the democratic system, and did not seek the destruction either of the system or of free enterprise. In Africa Black movements not only are prone to see violence as their salvation, but also frequently favor the destruction of the existing political and economic system and its replacement by a one-party Marxist set-up euphemistically known as "African socialism." Finally, there is what Barratt calls "the reality and strength of Afrikaner nationalism. No equivalent to that deeprooted resolution to maintain group identity and retain political power over the group's destiny, existed in the American South."

The inexperienced Georgian Mafia, however, is still blind to these differences. As the Washington Correspondent of *The Star,* Johannesburg, Eugene Hugo, has reported: "What Mr. Vorster now faces is an African policy charged with soaring rhetoric and infused with the moral fervor of the civil rights campaign—a policy designed to sweep away American mistakes of the past and make the American people 'feel good.' "

A policy hostile to South Africa is also being argued in terms of hardheaded realism. The deteriorating security situation in Southern Africa is interpreted as the inevitable result of increasing Black discontent with White tyranny. White Africa (so the prognosis in Washington goes) cannot resist this, and indeed is crumbling remarkably quickly (evidence is the South African pull-out from Rhodesia, and Namibia). As Black rule is inevitable in South Africa, it makes sense for the U.S. to ensure that it is associated with the "wave of the future," and doesn't again find itself backing a certain loser, as it did in South Vietnam. The U.S. should build alliances with "sound" governments, not find itself associated with unpopular, undemocratic, and therefore inherently unstable regimes.

Besides, "White tyranny" in Southern Africa is seen as a positive encouragement to Soviet ambitions, because it drives Black opinion to the Left, stimulates radical movements, prepares the ground for revolution, and unites Black Africa in a bloc more easily manipulated by Moscow. Inevitably, the United States' refusal till now to "lean" on White Africa, except by means of token gestures, is seen by Black Africa as secret support for the White governments. Hostility toward South Africa would show American concern with human rights. It would appeal to the Third World. It would even

16

offer an opportunity to undermine Soviet gains in Africa by gaining some sympathy among Black Marxists—sympathy that could then be strengthened by American aid in economic development. This is the rationale propounded in Washington.

There are also some material considerations. U.N. Ambassador Andrew Young has argued that as Black Africa is growing economically faster than White Africa, America's business interests would best be served by cultivating Black Africa. Secretary Vance has said: "Our trade with Nigeria alone is double the value of that with South Africa." For political as well as business reasons, the U.S. is keen to develop its links with Black Africa, and particularly with Nigeria, the giant of Black Africa. Nigeria is implacably opposed to South Africa.

It has also been suggested by the well-known South African journalist Aida Parker, quoting an unnamed South African banker, that "board members of the largest U.S. banks argue quite cynically that they could negotiate far more easily with a weak and possibly corrupt Black government in Pretoria than they can with a strong White one; that they could buy more cheaply from such a Black government, or simply take what they need, as Russia is doing in the African countries under its influence."

The domestic political advantages to the Carter Administration of a noisy campaign against South Africa would be considerable. It would enable Carter—a very sharp, flexible and able politician who is already being spoken of as another Franklin D. Roosevelt—to "guard his back" against loss of vital political support of Blacks and White liberals which he needs in Congress, and which he will need to secure his re-election in 1980.

Carter has seriously disappointed these groups by the conservatism of his financial policies. For instance Vernon Jordan, leader of the National Urban League, a prominent Black organization, has said that "many Black people feel that their hopes and their needs have been betrayed by President Jimmy Carter." A leader of the National Association for the Advancement of Colored Peoples, Margaret Bush Wilson, has attacked the President's goal of a balanced budget as "harmful to the interests of Blacks" because, for instance, it seemed to conflict with higher spending on public housing. She felt compelled "to remind President Carter that millions of people poured out of rat-infested, dilapidated, tenement houses from one end of the country to the other to give him his margin of victory." Gerald Ford actually beat Carter by a 51-to-48 ratio among Whites, but the 82 per cent of Blacks who voted for Carter gave him his narrow victory.

There is an underlying trend within the U.S. toward conservatism. This is reflected in the popularity of tightfisted financial policies pursued not only by President Carter, but also by people like Governor Jerry Brown of California; in the willingness of Congress to go for higher defense spending and support for "get tough" policies toward the Soviet Union; in a backlash over moral issues, such as the confinement of sex shops and other pornographic facilities to "combat zones" and an anti-homosexual vote in Florida's most liberal county; and in political moves and court decisions blocking and even reversing the tide of civil rights measures, which had started to reach a point of absurdity.

This swing to the Right will not necessarily help South Africa. On the contrary. The more Carter has to shift ground on domestic issues to please middle-of-the-roaders and conservatives (30 per cent of conservatives voted for Carter in 1976), the more he will need issues on which he can act to please Blacks and White liberals. Human rights is an obvious choice, as it is, in the words of a consultant who worked for liberals George McGovern in 1972 and Morris Udall in 1976, "perhaps the most important liberal issue." And South Africa is the most obvious target in the human rights area. "It is the one area where Carter can afford to play domestic politics without damaging U.S. foreign policy interests," says Professor Robert A. Price of Berkeley, California. "It's the perfect football, because there are many domestic reasons to be against South Africa, and none to be for South Africa."

Many would disagree with the final part of that statement. But it is true that President Carter could safely pursue a more hostile policy toward South Africa without generating significant domestic opposition.

18

2.

Washington's demands

What is it that the U.S. actually wants from South Africa? South Africans naturally want to know what they are expected to do to ward off the threatened wrath. Yet the Carter Administration has been infuriatingly vague about this. In meetings with South African Government officials, its policymakers have consistently refused to be drawn into explaining exactly what it is they want.

The gist of what they have told the South Africans is this: "We expect you to present to us a blueprint and a timetable for political, economic and social change. We shall then decide if they are acceptable to us. If they are, then we shall monitor your progress. If you speed up the pace of change, we shall 'reward' you by easing off some of the pressure. If you move too slowly for us, we shall 'punish' you by increasing the pressure." Secretary Vance has put it more elegantly and tactfully in a public speech in which he called for "a progressive transformation of South African society,"—which would mean "a new course toward full political participation by all South Africans"— but "the specific form of government through which this participation could be expressed is a matter for the people of South Africa to decide. There are many ways."

In its early days, the Carter Administration demanded an early transition to "majority rule"—Ambassador Young spoke of achieving this within a period of 18 months to 4 years. But South Africans, including prominent liberals as well as Government spokesmen, quickly asked what was meant by this phrase, as hardly anywhere in Africa is there rule by a political majority. Such a majority could only be shown by free democratic elections, which is an aspect of American life that does not appeal to most African rulers. Therefore the U.S. Administration could only be talking about a majority defined by race, which is an inherently racist concept. Perhaps it was just coincidence, but the Administration suddenly muted its calls for "majority rule" and began demanding instead "full participation" of Blacks in South Africa's political, economic and social life.

This phrase, in itself, is quite meaningless. South African Government supporters can argue quite reasonably that Blacks already participate fully in terms of the separate development policy and to the extent that they are able, given their level of cultural development. Blacks, Coloreds and Asians all have the vote in electing their own representative bodies. Most of these have a territorial base (homeland), where their authority ranges from limited self-government (Qwa-Qwa) to total independence (Transkei). There is an ongoing process of advancing political power to these bodies—for instance the Bophuthatswana homeland plans to become independent on December 6, 1977.

All the representative bodies speak for the interests of their ethnic communities in matters of day-to-day administration and in negotiations with the White-elected Government that is still the sovereign authority over all South Africa except Transkei. The Transkeian Government represents the interests of its many citizens still working within the Republic, in exactly the same way that the Italian, Spanish and Turkish governments represent the interests of their citizens working in West Germany.

In addition, these bodies are consulted by the White Government on broader issues of policy affecting the South African communities as a group (such as foreign affairs and defense). Admittedly, their influence in such matters is still very limited. But it is growing. And it has been made clear that their influence will be extended considerably in terms of a new structure of government now being worked out by a Cabinet Committee headed by Defense Minister Pieter W. Botha.

However, this kind of "full participation" is obviously not what the Carter Administration has in mind. Secretary Vance has said that the U.S. opposes the homelands policy because it "was devised without reference to the wishes of the Blacks themselves" (this is not true, as in several free elections Black ethnic groups have voted strongly for separate development), and "because we do not believe it constitutes a fair and viable solution to South Africa's problems." Vice-President Mondale has specifically rejected not only the South African system of Black participation as it exists, but the very basis on which it had developed over 300 years. "Separateness," he has said emphatically, is "inherently discriminatory."

This is all rather confusing from an Administration that is trying to force Israel to create a homeland for Palestinians—and has never suggested that their separateness from Israelis should be overcome by incorporating them within a single integrated political system, in which Arabs would outvote Jews and Israel's Jewish character would be destroyed. As recently as 1976 the U.S. itself partitioned its trust territory of Micronesia in the Pacific on what Donald McHenry, now a top Administration negotiator on Southern Africa, called "shaky legal and political grounds."

The clearest indication of the kind of political change the U.S. would like to see in South Africa came from Vice-President Mondale after his Vienna talks with Prime Minister Vorster in May, 1977. He told a Press conference that what the U.S. wanted was "full participation by all the citizens of South Africa," which he defined as "equal participation in the election of its national government and in its political affairs." This, he explained, was "the same thing as one man, one vote. Every citizen should have the right to vote and every vote should be equally weighed."

This hit South Africa like a bombshell. For such a dispensation would not merely end White domination over Blacks and discrimination against them (which an increasing number of South African Whites accept as inevitable). It would impose Black domination over Whites within an integrated system. Whites understandably fear that this would be a case of "one man, one vote, once," and that South Africa would go the way of most countries in Africa that have passed into the hands of Black rulers—a one-party state, muzzling of the Press, destruction of free enterprise, corruption, and sometimes much worse. It was like asking Israel to subject itself to the Arab League. Or saying that Americans should subject themselves to a United Nations' world government dominated by an alliance of the Afro-Asians and the Communists—a global version of majority rule.

This is why the South African reaction was outrage. Said Foreign Minister Botha: "If the United States demands the introduction of a political dispensation which must inevitably lead to our destruction, then we are on a collision course." Later he was to say in West Germany that "never in a hundred years" would Whites share power with Blacks (by inference, within an integrated political system). And in Australia he said bitterly: "The world wants one change and one change only—that we must accept our suicide joyfully."

Mondale's one man, one vote formula was immediately rejected by opponents as well as supporters of apartheid. It was seen as a demand so extreme in the South African context that it would unite the Whites, and undermine moderate forces for change within the country.

The eminent liberal writer Alan Paton, who has been honored worldwide for his unyielding opposition to apartheid, warned that if President Carter tried to pressure South Africa into early majority rule, the result would be the destruction of the country ... "its cities, its railways, its industries, its medicine, its agriculture." Ken Owen, probably South Africa's best-informed journalist on American affairs, said that U.S. pressure "might, in the end, drive us into a siege economy, collapse our remaining civil rights, spread misery and chaos," yet "not even then be likely to bring down the South African Government."

The most able and articulate of the country's liberal writers, former Rand Daily Mail editor Laurence Gandar, said that "by cutting the ground from under the feet of the moderates on both sides, who believe that White and Black have got to work together ... the protagonists of majority rule are presenting a formula for conflict, not conciliation." Tertius Myburgh, the liberal editor of the country's largest-circulation newspaper, the *Sunday Times,* commented that "whatever the motivation, the posing of alternatives in such stark terms is not going to help the cause of peaceful change in South Africa. It will simply raise emotional temperatures on all sides." It would "laagerize"* the Whites, help premier Vorster to

*When White settlers moving into the interior of South Africa in the 19th century were attacked by Black tribes, they circled their wagons into a "laager," put all their people within this protective barrier, and fired at their attackers, usually driving them off.

22

control the dissidents within his own party pushing for change, and raise too quickly the expectations of Blacks. It would limit the Government's ability to maneuver and damage the position of the Government's opponents—for instance by giving substance to the jibe frequently made at the Progressive Reform Party (the most liberal of the groups with substantial White support) that "even your policies will never satisfy the Carter crowd."

The problem with the punitive technique that the U.S. appeared to be adopting was, as another eminent South African journalist, Stephen Orpen, said in the news magazine *To The Point,* that it's "the way to make a man dig his heels in ... The way to stop him cooperating even when it is in his own best interests. If he's proud, threaten to punish a man unless he does something, and he is sure not to do it."

Even within the Administration there seemed to be those with grave doubts about the wisdom of Boer-bashing. National Security Council chief Dr. Zbigniew Brzezinski said: "We know from our own national experience that social rearrangements, particularly when they involve racial relations, are extremely difficult, extremely painful and cannot be achieved overnight. We also know that if the process begins, it is best to encourage it by praising, by approving what is being done, and by encouraging it to become more rapid—rather than by either pointing the gun at somebody's head or condemning him because he hasn't transformed himself over- night."

Since the Vienna Press conference, Administration spokesmen have been busily and emphatically denying, publicly and privately, that the U.S. wants one man, one vote, in South Africa. This infers that Mondale didn't know what he was talking about. This is hardly likely, as he is the Administration's top policymaker on Africa, he is no "blabbermouth" like Ambassador Young, and what he said was fully consistent with views on South Africa that have been expressed publicly and privately by his fellow policymakers.

The only reasonable explanation for this confusion is that the Administration's eventual political objective is indeed one man, one vote in South Africa. But that some influential members of the Administration, probably including the President himself, are perturbed that public talk about this will alienate the White liberals and moderates in South Africa, and drive the Whites into unified resistance to American pressure.

23

Many Whites disagree strongly with the South African Government's policies, and would sympathize with moves to bring about political rights and greater socio-economic progress for Blacks, Coloreds and Asians within a single political system and along the road to an integrated multiracial society. But hardly any of them would support a call for one man, one vote, either immediately or soon.

The Carter Administration has given little public indication of what specific changes it would like to see in the economic and social aspects of South Africa's race relations. President Carter himself has said: "We feel that there ought to be some equality of living practises, equality of pay for the same work done, promotion opportunities for Black citizens and an end to the highly discriminatory pass system." Vice-President Mondale has criticized "detention of political prisoners." Jim Srodes, a Washington journalist who reports for the South African Press, has written that "formal recognition of Black labor unions" is one desired change that is frequently mentioned. But the whole thrust of the Carter Administration's pressure so far has been for political change, presumably on the not unreasonable assumption that if Blacks had full political rights they would control South Africa, and if they did that they would quickly rid the country of all other forms of discrimination against them.

Several conclusions are possible about the U.S. Administration's infuriating vagueness about how it expects South Africa to provide these political rights. One is that Carter and his men really haven't the faintest idea how South Africa's complex racial problem should be solved, and about the only thing they know for certain is that they don't like Pretoria's current approach. Another is that the Administration is deeply divided within itself and cannot agree on a solution. It was reported in February 1977 that in a briefing for Congressmen, National Security Adviser Brzezinski declared that separate development (the South African Government's concept of separation) was the only solution to the racial problems of South Africa, at which point Ambassador Young interrupted heatedly: "No way."

A third possibility is that the Administration knows exactly what it wants—rapid progress to majority rule within a unitary state, but feels it will get more concessions out of the South African Government, and will keep White opinion within South Africa disunited, by keeping this quiet. A fourth explanation is that the

Administration doesn't really care about constitutional niceties, as all it really wants is Blacks in power, fast, in the national interests of the U.S. and the political interests of the Administration. It would also establish a precedent for interference in the internal affairs of other countries, such as Israel.

3.

Carter's limited freedom of action

Despite the signs that the Carter Administration is moving toward a much more hostile policy on South Africa—and we can expect to see practical evidence of this in the closing months of 1977—there is no clarity about what Carter will do, how far he will go. Many of the specific measures that have been mentioned are of such a magnitude, and have such serious implications for the U.S. and for other countries, that they look more like empty threats than real possibilities.

There are many built-in brakes on any trend towards extreme measures against South Africa. The first and most important of these is likely to be President Carter himself. Carter is no extremist. Indeed, whether from conviction or from political opportunism, he is generally about as moderate and as middle-of-the-road as you can get within the spectrum of American political opinion. He believes in pressure rather than brute force, and while threatening South Africa with tough measures constitutes pressure, implementing those measures would amount to brute force.

According to political scientist Donald G. Baker, Carter believes that material human rights, such as "the individual's right to food, shelter, clothing and employment" take precedence over civil and political rights. If this is correct, and Carter initially stresses improvement in the economic and living conditions of South African Blacks, then he could hardly opt for most of the tough economic measures that his Administration has threatened to apply, as these would make impossible any improvements in Blacks' economic and living conditions.

Carter is known to be worried about the Western world's economic malaise, and must realize that politically-inspired measures that savaged one of the world's more important medium-sized economies and trading nations, and consequently damaged its trading partners (particularly U.S. allies in Europe), would hardly help in the search for a cure for that malaise. Carter is also known to be keen to aid the emergence of a large, free enterprise-orientated Black middle class in South Africa. Economic sanctions would retard that process, and radicalize the existing Black middle class.

Then there is the influence of the moderates who surround Carter in his Administration, like Secretary of State Cyrus Vance and NSC chief Zbigniew Brzezinski. Not all his team, by any means, are Blacks, ultra-liberals, inexperienced bright young men from Georgia with instant solutions to the world's problems, or macchiavellians who view Southern Africa in simplistic terms of backing "inevitable" Black winners.

Some of the insiders give some weight to the South African arguments that the Republic is a counterbalance to Soviet power in the Southern African region, and that weakening it by economic sanctions and military embargoes would play Moscow's game. Some acknowledge the critical importance of certain Southern African minerals to the industry of the West and of Japan, and do not accept that these materials would automatically be available, or available on reasonable terms, should the region dissolve into chaos or pass under the control of pro-Soviet governments.

Some accept that access to South Africa's ports and airfields has a strategic significance for the U.S. in relation to the Cape sea route and the Middle East. Some doubt the validity of the prognosis that the South African Government will be easily and quickly toppled by a combination of internal revolution and external pressures. Some accept that one man, one vote, within a single unitary state, is no solution to the South African problem, and argue that a better course would be a more advanced form of separate development —an ethnic confederation or even radical partition into Black and

White states. Some are particularly conscious of the limits on the United States' power to reshape foreign societies according to American values and traditions.

It is impossible for an outsider, or perhaps even for an insider, to predict with any degree of certainty the extent to which the moderate influences within the Administration will neutralize the radical influences in shaping Carter's mind for the final decisions on measures to be taken against South Africa. For the final decisions in such an important matter will undoubtedly be the President's.

At present the radicals appear to be dominant in foreign policy making, and as a result the U.S. is experiencing setbacks in its foreign relations around the world. Carter is too clever, adaptable, and sensitive to political realities, not to react to these setbacks, so in time one can expect the moderates to gain influence in this sphere. We could see Vance either gain stature or leave the Administration to make way for a stronger man (perhaps energy czar James Schlesinger?). We could see Brzezinski ("Carter's Kissinger"), gain in power just as Kissinger did in the Nixon Administration. We could see the highly intelligent Mondale become more important in Southern African policymaking, to the detriment of the highly emotional Young.

A few words about the remarkable Ambassador Young, the Congregationalist minister from Georgia—former Congressman, righthand man of Martin Luther King, and now President's confidant in the Carter Cabinet. Young is an even more controversial figure in South Africa than he is in the U.S. When he visited the country in May 1977 one of his more remarkable statements was that the life span of Blacks in Rhodesia was half that of Whites owing to infant mortality, disease and malnutrition caused by systematic oppression and death dealing, and that this was also true of South Africa, with "minor qualifications". Logically, therefore, if all the Whites departed and thus ended the "systematic oppression and death dealing," infant mortality, disease and malnutrition would all decline sharply. In fact, as anyone who knows anything about Africa would realize, the very opposite would happen—as it did in Angola and Mozambique. In fact the health standards of Blacks in White-ruled countries are very much higher than those most places else on the continent. Young was talking nonsense to appeal to a Black audience which is all too often willing to listen to the kind of claptrap that does nothing to improve race relations in

Africa. It was a fast crack to gain instant applause.

Young is also an apologist for the Soviet bloc's expansionism in Africa, having suggested that the Cuban forces in Angola are a "steadying influence." He had no objections to the first draft of a U.N. resolution in June 1977 that would have legitimized landing of Soviet bloc troops in Mozambique, to "protect" that country against attacks from Rhodesia (which only occur because Mozambique allows its territory to be used for terrorist bases for operations against Rhodesia—in international law, an act of war).

Young says he opposes violence, yet he excuses it. For instance he accepts the rationale of the terrorist movements that all kinds of abominable atrocities are permissible against civilians (usually Black) because they are "only responding to White governments' institutionalized violence." His actual words were: "There is a sense in which the oppressive racist regimes are being aggressively violent. Frelimo did not organize the armed struggle until 600 people who were doing nothing were shot down." Americans, of course, can be expected to sympathize with rebellion against tyranny in view of their proud history. But to equate terrorist gangs with the Revolutionary Army would be an insult. The Revolutionary Army did not carry out sadistic atrocities in order to win, and it fought for democracy and freedom, not Marxist dictatorship.

Notwithstanding all this, Young is a charismatic and personally likeable man, with a gift for dramatic phrases (even if they don't stand up to logical analysis). One can see why President Carter chose him as a kind of "point man" or chief public relations officer to promote the U.S. and outbid the Soviet Union in the Third World. He talks the kind of nonsense that is popular at the United Nations. Trouble is, in doing so, he upsets the more sophisticated countries. Nations like Britain and Sweden understandably don't like being classified as racist. Because of their pasts, they are rather sensitive about such accusations. Then there are many countries, particularly the important ones, who don't believe in Young-style open diplomacy because their experience convinces them that it never succeeds.

Why does President Carter put up with him? According to that pillar of liberal wisdom, *The Washington Post*, which has said he should be fired, Carter won't do so because he suffers from a guilt complex because he was slow to rally to the cause of racial justice in the South. He feels a disciple's respect and humility before an apostle.

It seems to me that South Africans place undue importance on Ambassador Young's role in shaping U.S. policy toward South Africa. Many conclude that he is such a blabbermouth that he cannot last, and then when he goes, the pressure on South Africa will ease. Others are convinced that he is so close to the President that he is the dominant force in making policy, and will stay that way. I take a middle view. I believe that Young is close enough to Carter to be an important influence, but not a dominating one. If he is shifted—and the President has already told him not to allow Africa to monopolize his time, but to give attention to other Third World areas such as Latin America, the Caribbean and Asia—it will make little difference to the Administration's South Africa policy. There are too many others close in there who believe in it.

If the Carter Administration reverts to a more "responsible" and pragmatic foreign policy generally, that would not necessarily let South Africa off the hook. On the contrary. Vice-President Mondale, for instance, would be a far shrewder and more influential opponent of the South African Government than Young. South Africa would remain a suitable "football" for Carter's domestic political purposes.

However there would be factors outside the Administration which could act as a brake should President Carter choose to pursue strongly anti-South African courses of action. One of the most important would be Congress. Some of the measures South Africa is being threatened with would require an Act of Congress—for instance those involving any appropriation of funds. Others (such as U.S. Treasury gold sales) could be implemented by executive order. Others again by quietly-exercised bureaucratic pressure. However, Congress could prohibit executive action and stop the bureaucrats by resolution, provided it could muster a two-thirds majority to override any consequent presidential veto.

Of course the President has considerable power to get what he wants, even from Congress, if he is prepared to pay a high enough price. There are many material favors that he can grant which, in a crunch, can outweigh the sympathies of Congressmen and Senators, or the opinions and direct interests of their constituents. But would clobbering South Africa be worth a high price? The Congress is, overall, politically more conservative than the Administration. And it is (as a result of the way the U.S. gotten involved in Vietnam by presidential maneuvering) much more conscious of its power to restrain the President's freedom of action in the foreign policy area than it has been traditionally, and much more inclined to exercise that power.

External factors are likely to prove the most effective restraints on implementation of extreme measures against South Africa. For instance mandatory sanctions prohibiting trade by any of the world's 160-odd states with the Republic would only be possible if none of the 5 veto-carrying powers represented on the U.N. Security Council imposed its veto to block the passing of an appropriate resolution. The Communist powers, Russia and China, obviously would not (they have proved in the case of Rhodesia that they are willing to support sanctions publicly while secretly continuing to trade). If the U.S. chose not to exercise its veto as well, this would leave the decision up to Britain and France.

France has in the past been more friendly toward South Africa than the other powers. For instance it continued to supply advanced weaponry when the U.S., Britain and West Germany refused, and it aided rather than hampered its industrialists' (ultimately successful) efforts to win the contract to build the Republic's first nuclear power station in competition with American, German, Dutch and Swiss interests. But France, probably because it is coming round to the view that White South Africa will collapse like White Algeria rather than resist like Israel, has been moving slowly toward a more hostile attitude on South Africa. It has promised to supply no more weapons when present contracts expire. There is also a trend toward the Left in France's domestic policies, which could lead to a Socialist-Communist alliance gaining power in 1978. What's more, its business with South Africa is not large compared with its dealings with the rest of Africa and its foreign trade as a whole. The chances are increasing that, if the U.S. chose to pursue a policy of trade sanctions, France would not stymie it (at least publicly—like the Communist powers, it secretly trades with Rhodesia).

Britain's situation is quite different, however. South Africa was in 1976 Britain's fourth largest export market outside Europe, buying significantly more than Iran or Saudi Arabia, almost twice as much as Japan and more than $2\frac{1}{2}$ times more than the Soviet Union. Sales to the Republic were worth $1.1-billion, and it has been estimated that at least 100,000 British jobs depend on this trade. Britain also has several billion dollars' worth of profitable investments in South

Africa and this, combined with the traditional links with the two countries, produces a huge flow of "invisible earnings"—dividends, interest, and earnings from shipping and insurance services—worth probably another $1-billion or more every year. Sanctions would not only cost Britain its earnings from South Africa, but would also force it to buy elsewhere the $1-billion worth of goods that it now imports from the Republic. Inevitably, their cost would be higher —an additional burden that could run to several hundreds of millions of dollars a year. Britain traditionally has a weak balance of payments, and could not afford to destroy its economic links with South Africa.

If Britain did not veto a trade sanctions resolution, it would have to comply with it, and would probably do so more honestly than most other countries. This would do grave damage to the British economy. Foreign Secretary Dr. David Owen has already intimated that his government would not be willing to do that. If a moderate Labor Government holds that view it is unlikely that a Conservative Government, which looks set to take power in 1978, would be any more willing to countenance sanctions. It is true that pressure from the U.S. and from Black Africa, which is gaining in economic importance for the British, could put London in a cruel dilemma. But it could probably expect significant support from its European allies, especially West Germany, which is conscious of Western Europe's economic dependence on South Africa. Bonn is already unhappy about the extent to which it has to "subsidize" its partners in the EEC, and fears that it would have to pick up a large part of the tab for damage done to European economies by any sanctions against South Africa.

American policymakers who threatened the South African Government with U.S. trade sanctions said that they would induce the British to go along with them by promising a U.S.-provided compensatory financing facility to offset the huge losses that Britain would suffer from a boycott. But it does not seem credible that President Carter, a fiscal conservative, whose country faces its own worsening balance of payments problem, would countenance such a commitment. It is even less likely that the Congress would be willing to authorize expenditure on such a scale. The British would certainly expect grants (not loans) in excess of $2-billion a year. And other countries would undoubtedly demand equivalent treatment. All this, just to be nasty to South Africa? It does not seem possible.

For the foreseeable future, the threat of worldwide mandatory sanctions against South Africa must surely be an empty one.

4.

Real and unreal
dangers

Among the many sanctions the Republic has been threatened with, the most frightening to ordinary South Africans is that of an oil embargo. Yet careful analysis indicates that this is one of the least likely options that the Carter Administration would resort to because of practical difficulties. And that even if it were applied, it would not have the devastating or conclusive effects that many believe.

An oil boycott could not be implemented with certainty without a naval blockade of South Africa's coastline, which (with the Transkei's coast) extends 1,836 miles from Ponta do Ouro on the Indian Ocean to the mouth of the Orange River on the Atlantic. In addition, the Republic still controls the 900-mile coastline of Namibia, including the port of Walvis Bay (which is an enclave of South African territory). The waters along these coasts are rough, vast in extent, and remote from the developed nations. A naval blockade would be needed for several years for an oil boycott to have any real punitive effect, and this would require the commitment of substantial military and financial resources. It is unlikely that it would be possible, politically, for the U.S. to mount such a blockade with its Navy alone. Nor could it countenance the Soviet

Navy handling such a responsibility. Therefore it would require a major exercise in international collaboration of a kind for which there is no precedent. That looks most unlikely.

The Administration could of course try to organize an unpoliced international oil embargo. This would require the cooperation of all oil exporters, and especially of the two largest, Iran and Saudi Arabia. These countries are both conservative, strongly anti-Communist, in varying degrees sympathetic toward South Africa, and not easily manipulated by the Americans because of the freedom of action that their oil power provides. Even if oil suppliers all publicly agreed to a boycott, it is unlikely that it would be effective. Communist states have consistently breached international sanctions applied against Rhodesian chrome. It is unlikely they would be able to resist selling oil at a high price to South Africa to breach any embargo (according to one London source, they actually did so in 1973 when the international oil boycott was also applied to the Republic).

Even if South Africa were totally cut off from foreign oil, it would be inconvenienced rather than crippled. It has huge strategic oil stocks, believed to be sufficient for several years' usage at normal rates of consumption, and considerably more on a rationed basis. It is only dependent on petroleum for one-fourth of its energy needs. It has one oil-from-coal plant operational and another much larger one under construction. And it could quickly build plants to manufacture huge quantities of methanol, synthetic natural gas, and other substitutes for conventional liquid fuels. South Africa has a great deal of experience with alcohol fuels and Brazil, which is planning to make these on a huge scale from sugarcane, is partially basing its initiative on this experience.

What about another offensive against gold? This would bring the U.S. into conflict with European allies which, notwithstanding the official international demonetization of gold brought about by U.S. initiative, still like to keep substantial quantities of bullion in their monetary reserves. They see gold as an asset that, unlike paper currencies, cannot be used to perpetrate international fraud. There is no limit to which the U.S. can "print" dollars, thus lowering the real value of all existing dollars held in international reserves, provided it is prepared to accept the inflationary consequences. Gold cannot be "manufactured" at whim.

These allies would be outraged if the U.S. sought to smash the price of gold just to be nasty to the South Africans. France and Italy alone, for instance, have between them about $25-billion worth of gold, at current market values, in their official reserves. They would lose close to $2-billion for every $10 drop in the free market price. In addition, the gold price is a political issue in France, where private holdings run to many billions, while France in turn has great influence within the European Economic Community—America's most important, powerful and reliable ally. The gold price has particular importance for Italy, which has pledged part of its gold holdings as collateral for loans. It has some importance for West Germany (which has billions of dollars worth in its official reserves, and made the loans to Italy against that country's gold pledge); for Switzerland (whose banks' stability, and with it probably the stability of the international banking system, depends partially on the value of their gold stocks, and their clients , holding up); and for The Netherlands (two-thirds of whose reserves are in gold, if the bullion is valued at free market price).

Nevertheless, this situation is not very different from what it has been in the past. Yet in the past the U.S. has been able to pursue its campaign against gold with some success. So a further limited offensive, perhaps excused as a balance of payments-protecting measure to obviate the need to import gold for industrial purposes, or perhaps excused as a counter-attack to protect the weakening dollar against "international speculators," cannot be ruled out. Treasury stocks, as Antony C. Sutton points out in his book "The War on Gold," are equal to about 12 times South Africa's annual gold output. Even though Washington could hardly go as far as dumping the entire contents of Fort Knox on the world market, auction of several million ounces, accompanied by a fanfare of anti-gold propaganda, would disrupt the international bullion market and drive down the gold price. Every dollar drop in the price, if sustained over a 12-month period, costs South Africa more than $20-million a year in lost foreign exchange earnings.

About the easiest to implement of the major measures that South Africa is being threatened with by the Carter Administration, would be "turning off the tap" through which foreign investment flows into the Republic. This would do more than just diminish South Africa's foreign exchange inflow. It would also diminish the country's access to advanced nations' technology and managerial knowhow, which tend to "ride on the back" of greenbacks, and which have traditionally been important factors in South Africa's economic development.

Although the U.S. could not stop flow of capital into South Africa from other countries, such as Switzerland and West Germany, it could diminish that flow considerably, both by means of diplomatic pressure on the governments of the countries concerned, and by "demonstration effect." Private companies in Europe and elsewhere would be reluctant to incur the wrath of the U.S. Government, notwithstanding the profitability of investment in South Africa, and they would tend to interpret U.S. action as evidence of the risk of civil disorder, even revolution, in Southern Africa.

A number of ways have been suggested of "turning off the tap". The more mandatory they become, the more they conflict with America's free enterprise traditions. And the more they damage U.S. corporate interests, the more difficult they would be to apply, of course. Here they are. They are ranked from the easiest to the most difficult for the Administration to implement:

- Apply discreet pressure on corporations invested in South Africa, Namibia or Rhodesia, or even merely trading with the 3 countries, by hints that the Federal Government will make life difficult for them—and there are many ways it can do so—unless they stop investing in Southern Africa.

- Generate public pressure on the corporations involved, and give tacit support to the anti-South African lobby, by publicizing the names and activities of those involved, and escalating the magnitude and intensity of political criticism of their activities.

- Get Congress to pass a resolution that, while not outlawing additional investment in South Africa, discourages it. This would be as effective as an outright ban as far as many companies are concerned.

- Rescind quotas, trade preferences and other advantages enjoyed by U.S. corporations doing business with the Republic.

- Stop awarding Federal Government contracts, and/or export/import licences, to U.S. companies doing business with South Africa.

- Disallow, as deductions from U.S. tax liabilities, taxes paid by U.S. corporations' South African subsidiaries to the South

African Government. This would gravely damage the profitability of existing or planned investments in the Republic.

● Outright prohibition of additional U.S. investment in South Africa, in the same way as such investment is banned in Rhodesia and Cuba.

The American offensive against South Africa is certainly coming at a particularly awkward time for the men in Pretoria who control the nation's destinies. After almost 30 years in power, with polls showing an alltime high in level of voter support, the ruling National Party should be supremely selfconfident, even complacent, with a firm hand on the affairs of state. But it is far from that. Politically, economically and militarily, the country is beset with problems. Internally and externally, there are unprecedented challenges.

Politically, it is a time of confusion and uncertainty. Within the ruling establishment there is a gargantuan struggle going on for supremacy between the liberals and conservatives on the issues of race, which are the issues that have long dominated South African politics. The liberals *(verligtes)* want much faster dismantling of the structure of legalized racial discrimination, speeded-up consolidation of the Black-primacy territories ("Homelands") into cohesive and viable entities, and decisions on a firm plan for a new constitutional system which would bring Coloreds, Asians, even Blacks, into the decisionmaking processes of government for the country as a whole. The conservatives *(verkramptes)* oppose such proposals as too radical, unnecessary, even violations of the fundamental principles of the ruling party, and likely to stimulate rather than dampen revolutionary pressures.

There is also a struggle between the hawks and the doves (not necessarily identifiable with liberals and conservatives, as many liberals are hawks and some conservatives are doves), on defense and foreign policy issues. The hawks, for instance, argue for a "forward defense" with South African military involvement in Rhodesia, while the doves would like to "cut off the water" and force the Smith Government to capitulate, removing Rhodesia as an embarrassment in South Africa's international relations.

Present South African policies are uncomfortable compromises between the viewpoints of the various camps within the establishment, with the conservatives still dominant on race issues but losing ground, and the doves still dominant on defense/foreign issues, but also losing ground.

On the Left, the White opposition, once united and powerful, has disintegrated into 3 warring groups that look increasingly irrelevant, while on the Right the breakaway HNP (Re-established National Party) enjoys little support: there is no credible alternative, nor even effective opposition, to a ruling party starting to show some of the signs of having been too long in power.

The Black politicians are disorganized. The old radical leaders are jailed, banished or exiled. The new radicals are inexperienced and notably extreme (Soweto leader Tsietsi Mashinini says that all South Africa's 4.3-million Whites must leave the African continent or they will be slaughtered). The moderate leaders are split over the issue of whether they should sabotage or collaborate with, and exploit, the Government's separate development policies. The ablest, like Zulu leader Gatsha Buthelezi, drift towards a militancy which holds their support among Blacks but undermines their power to influence the Whites, who control the country's political destiny.

Economically, South Africa is reeling from the punishment of its worst recession since the Thirties, with business confidence gravely weakened and unemployment approaching, and perhaps already exceeding, the 2-million mark. The primary cause was the international recession associated with the massive rise in oil prices. This plunged South Africa into a balance of payments crisis ... like all other developing and semi-developed countries depending on export of commodities for most of its foreign exchange earnings and having to import their oil.

Other factors extended the economic damage. One was the collapse of the price of gold, partly as a result of a U.S. campaign to drive gold out of the international monetary system. Another was some bad economic management in Pretoria, where Government spending was allowed to get out of control and "the printing press" was used to finance it; over the 2 years 1973 and 1974 the money supply burgeoned 52 per cent, with scarcely a word of public criticism. A third factor was the deterioration in the external and internal security situation in Southern Africa, highlighted by the South African-Cuban clash in Angola and the rioting in Black townships that started in Soweto in June 1976—this damaged both foreign and domestic confidence in the economy, and obliged the Government to escalate defense spending.

As a result of all this, the current account of the balance of payments plunged deep into the red in 1974 with a deficit equivalent to $1.2-billion at today's dollar/rand rate of exchange, went even worse in 1975 with a gap of $2.1-billion, and was still in the red to the tune of $1.7-billion in 1976. Like Brazil, Mexico and similar countries well-regarded by international investors, South Africa borrowed heavily to offset these deficits. Long- and short-term capital movements netted out at a positive $1-billion in 1974 (calculated at today's rate of exchange), $2.2-billion in 1975 and $1.1-billion in 1976.

This borrowing process became harder as it proceeded. Many international financial institutions have long been unwilling to lend to South Africa on political grounds; the limited band willing to do so started excusing themselves, saying that their portfolios were as full of South African paper as they were willing to accept. Then came the South African political defeat in Angola, the sharp increase in Soviet influence in the area, the weak response of the South African authorities to the violence in the Black townships, and the first serious signs of impending collapse of White authority in neighboring Rhodesia. The whole situation in Southern Africa began to look destabilized. Not surprisingly, the Republic discovered it difficult to borrow more except at exorbitant rates of interest, while many nervous rich South Africans started to shift hundreds of millions, legally and illegally, out of the country to havens in Europe and North America. The South African Government had to scratch around for capital, doing "gold swaps" with Swiss banks that really amounted to gold pledges on loans, and making use of its credit lines at the IMF.

At the time of writing, in July, 1977, the South African economy was starting to show some positive signs, with the current account of the balance of payments moving towards surplus and a nil-growth situation in the money supply presaging a sharp fall in the rate of inflation. But on the whole, the economy still looked bleak; still sliding deeper into recession, without any improvement in the level of foreign reserves, unable to attract foreign capital, with inflation still raging and growing discontent among both Black and White work forces.

Militarily, the country is threatened by the build-up of Soviet influence in the region and escalating guerilla conflict in its buffer territories—Rhodesia and Namibia. The Cuban forces on whose bayonets the survival of Angola's MPLA government depends, are being strengthened. There are now thousands of Soviet bloc "advisers" in Mozambique. And Russian arms are pouring into both the former Portuguese territories. The Soviet Navy is strengthening its presence in the South Atlantic and Indian oceans. Rhodesia, the morale of its Whites seriously undermined by the commitment to majority rule, staggers under the burden of defense against external attack: its collapse would open up Botswana as a base area for terrorist armies and bring guerillas to an additional 2,000 miles of South African and Namibian frontier stretching from Pafuri in the North East Transvaal to Kazangula at the tip of the Caprivi Strip. The military are having to re-equip and re-train for possible conventional war as well as the long-prepared-for revolutionary war, while expanding established White units and developing the new Black, Colored and Asian units.

In its foreign relations, the Republic's isolation is increasing, for several reasons. One is the hostility of the new U.S. Administration. Another is that events in Southern Africa these past several years, and Pretoria's reactions to them, have led many foreigners to start to doubt the Republic's stability and its capacity to adapt to and/or resist external and internal pressures. A third reason is that, with the ending of the Vietnam war, South Africa has become the obvious target for Leftist groups worldwide, ranging from liberal humanists in search of a cause to Soviet agents seeking to promote their country's national interests.

The internal security situation also poses problems. An increasing number of Blacks interpret the events in Southern Africa since 1974 as presaging the collapse of the "White bastion" in South Africa, and are willing to lend an ear to those preaching violence to bring down the crumbling bastion from within, like the Trojan horse. Communist-backed revolutionary groups outside the country are stepping up their subversion within it. An ironic consequence of the Government's strenuous efforts to improve Black educational facilities in recent years is that the pool of young, educated, urban Blacks is growing rapidly larger ... and this Marxist-oriented group is the ideal material for revolutionary cadres. Doubts about the future that worry foreigners also erode the morale of White South Africa. Thousands from the business and professional classes have left or are planning to emigrate mainly to the U.S., Canada, Britain and Australia.

41

Against this background of escalating difficulties, it is understandable that South Africa's enemies conclude that the Republic is a push-over. It won't be.

5.

What South Africa can expect

Commonsense leads one to assume that President Carter will, at least initially, adopt the easy options on any hit list presented to him, in the hope that the South African Government will crumble under pressure as it has before. Therefore in the months ahead we can expect the U.S. Administration to step up its barrage of propaganda—through the media, at the United Nations, and via diplomatic activity—against African Whites and in favor of African Blacks. We can expect a rising tide of private and public criticism of U.S. corporations with Southern African involvements, with a tacit alliance emerging between the Administration and the growing anti-South African lobby.

And we can expect some concrete measures against South Africa of a token nature that will do little real damage to the Republic (except perhaps to morale), but will be intended to indicate America's determination to play it rough, if needs be. In this category are measures such as:

● Downgrading the level of U.S. diplomatic relations (Japan, for instance, already limits the status of its highest-ranking envoy in South Africa to consul-general, and will not either send an ambassador or receive one in Tokyo).

- Cutting remaining intelligence links (while continuing to enjoy access to South African-sourced information via NATO allies).
- Discouraging travel to South Africa (especially for tourism purposes) by American nationals, and imposing tougher visa limitations on South Africans wishing to visit the U.S. or settle in the country.
- Stepping up the "educational" campaign among South African Blacks by the U.S. Information Service, the Voice of America, and academic and pseudo-academic institutions.
- Banning Eximbank guarantees on trade loans for South Africa.

Should President Carter then decide really to turn on the heat, the more likely of the many possible measures that he could opt for would be:

- Asking Congress to pass a resolution discouraging additional corporate investment in, or bank loans to, South Africa.
- Renew Treasury gold sales, in combination with a new psychological offensive against gold.
- Refuse to use the U.S. veto at the U.N. on any resolution favoring economic sanctions against South Africa (but without any real pressure on Britain not to use its veto, which would therefore almost certainly be cast, and would continue to protect the Republic against mandatory embargoes).
- Extend the U.S. arms embargo to cover civilian equipment with possible military application, and put pressure on other countries to stop military collaboration with the Republic.

Less likely, but still possible, are measures such as these:

- Administrative action to discourage corporations from doing business with South Africa, including disallowance of tax credits.
- Start confiscating goods of Namibian origin, effectively preventing their import into the U.S.
- Pressure on the IMF to get tough over loans to South Africa.
- Start providing medical supplies and other non-military

assistance to Black revolutionary groups attempting the violent overthrow of White governments in Southern Africa.

● Refuse to process South African-sourced uranium into nuclear fuel for South Africa's customers.

● Notify intention to refuse to renew South African Airways' landing rights in New York when the existing agreement covering these rights expires in 1979.

The measures that President Carter is least likely to implement are the scary ones: a ban on imports into the U.S. from South Africa; pressure on Western European allies to bring about an effective worldwide trade boycott; oil sanctions; and freezing of South African-owned assets within the U.S.

There can be no doubt that a confrontation with the United States will exacerbate South Africa's many problems. Outside pressure will tend to polarize the conflicting groups within the ruling party. The outcome is uncertain as far as racial policies are concerned, but can hardly help the liberal faction. British Foreign Secretary David Owen has pointed out that "if we drive the White South Africans into a total laager mentality, we could force one of the most Right-wing and most loathsome regimes to develop." An understandable exaggeration. But he makes a valid point.

U.S. hostility will worsen the international political climate that South Africa is already experiencing, and thus discourage all further financial, economic and political commitments to South Africa by foreign interests. It will also damage the morale of private business within the country, which will be less inclined to invest and give momentum to recovery from recession. Specific economic sanctions such as cutting the flow of American corporate investment funds to South Africa, or launching an offensive against the gold price, would make it harder for the Republic to overcome its balance of payments problem. This would delay the point in time at which the authorities will be able to take the brakes off the economy, touch the throttle, and go for growth. It would also do considerable damage to the economies of Black states whose prosperity is closely integrated with South Africa, such as Botswana, Lesotho, Swaziland and Transkei ... even Mozambique, Zambia and Zaire.

The principal victims of such economic sanctions would be South Africa's Blacks, Coloreds and Asians. The growth in their living standards, which has been remarkable in recent years, would continue to slow down and might stop entirely. Unemployment would continue to rise, not so much because of retrenchment as because an additional quarter-million workers pour on to the labor market each year. Additional measures to educate and upgrade the disadvantaged would become more difficult to finance.

Increasing commitment by Washington to the Black cause could be expected to boost the morale of Black radicals seeking the overthrow of White authority in Southern Africa, and encourage them to violence, while encouraging the vast majority of Blacks who are moderate or apolitical, to start shifting toward support for these radicals.

Those are the negative aspects. But there are also a number of positive ones. For instance, threats or actions to isolate South Africa internationally have tended in the past to promote strategic self-sufficiency, and there is no reason to expect that the future will be any different. Ten years before OPEC was founded and 23 before it used its power for political ends, South Africa recognized the potential danger of oil sanctions (having no deposits of its own) and established the Sasol oil-from-coal plant. It is now the world leader in oil-from-coal technology and in the related technology of manufacture of synthetic natural gas from coal. In the Sixties and early Seventies the Republic bought huge quantities of crude oil for its strategic reserves, largely stored underground in bomb-proof reservoirs. When the world oil price quadrupled in 1973, it immediately showed a huge capital profit on its cheaply-bought stocks.

The principal effect of the arms embargo imposed on South Africa by the U.S. and Britain was to create a large and sophisticated arms industry within the country that now supplies 57 per cent of the defense equipment required (75 per cent if naval equipment is excluded), and has begun exporting to several other nations. Fears of isolation led South Africa to develop its own unique uranium enrichment technology.

The Republic has a remarkable potential for self-sufficiency, should it choose to develop along those lines or be forced to by international economic sanctions. It is more than selfsufficient in food, producing enough grains and protein foods for national requirements, as well as exporting substantial quantities of corn, sugar and fruit. Its only important food imports are the beverages coffee, tea and cocoa. But both coffee and tea are grown on a limited scale, and their cultivation could be extended. The country possesses every mineral required by modern industry except bauxite (aluminum ore), high grade magnesite (source of magnesium metal, and also used for steel furnace linings) and potash (a fertilizer ingredient). But according to Dr. Bill van Rensburg, Professor of Energy Economics at Johannesburg's Rand Afrikaans University, "research has indicated that all 3 could be produced from unconventional sources" (within South Africa) "at prices not very much in excess of those prevailing, should the need arise." South Africa has to import about 15-million tons of crude oil a year. But as I have already explained, it is less dependent on petroleum than other developed economies, and could survive total cut-off from external sources with a combination of rationing, drawing-down strategic reserves, oil-from-coal, and manufacture of substitute fuels.

South Africa's imports largely consist of capital goods and processed materials and components for its manufacturing industries, with consumer goods (including automobiles) only 14 per cent of the total. Hardly any of the items it imports could not be made within the Republic if it were necessary. Industrial development has already reached a relatively advanced level, with plants that manufacture to the microscopic tolerances required by the nuclear power and other precision engineering industries, produce tool steels and sophisticated drugs, and build computers, ships, railroad locomotives and mach-2 jet fighters. South Africa exports automobile components to more than 100 countries (including the U.S.), has some of the world's biggest plants in fields such as commercial explosives, insecticides and cutlery, and has scored important breakthroughs, for instance in inventing the tellurometer land surveying instrument (now used worldwide), the Schaffel high-speed railroad bogie, and the Cactus surface-to-air missile.

The major reason South Africa imports about two-thirds of its capital goods and one-half its intermediate goods requirements is that it is more economical to do so than to manufacture locally. The Rhodesian experience has shown how a country can survive trade sanctions. Rhodesia not only developed a high level of self-sufficiency on a tiny industrial base, but also produced an astonishing economic performance, with one of the world's highest growth rates in real terms and lowest rates of inflation. South Africa has a much greater potential for self-sufficiency than Rhodesia, because its industrial base is so much larger and more advanced. For instance a recent report by the Prime Minister's Scientific Adviser showed that 12 per cent of 1976 imports could be replaced immediately by local products, and a further 10 per cent could be replaced with some additional investment. Those potentials were calculated under comparatively normal trading conditions, not those of a siege economy.

South Africa is much less susceptible to sanctions against its exports than most countries, for several reasons. One is that almost half its foreign exchange is derived from precious minerals—gold, diamonds, platinum—that can be sold anywhere without identification of source, and could even be slipped through a blockade by aircraft, submarine or small boat.

Another is that the world could hardly do without certain of its resources without great inconvenience and cost—for instance, chrome, manganese and vanadium. A third reason is that the Republic has substantial exports to other African countries, many of which have shown that while they publicly demand sanctions, they privately prefer to carry on trading.

If Washington banned corporate investment in South Africa, Pretoria might well be forced to retaliate by prohibiting transfer abroad of dividends and interest by U.S.-controlled companies. As U.S. investments in the Republic are generally rather profitable, the foreign exchange saved each year in this way would offset to some extent the damage done by an investment ban.

Cutting off the flow of capital to South Africa would only have a limited effect. One reason is that the Republic has always been less dependent on foreign capital for its development than most developing and semi-developed countries, generating most of its capital needs from a high level of domestic savings. For instance, over the 5 years 1969 to 1973, net capital inflow from abroad financed only 10 per cent of gross domestic investment. The proportion increased sharply during the years 1974 to 1976, but this was partly because of huge infrastructural development projects like the Richards Bay and Sishen-Saldanha schemes, which are approaching completion and are better than self-financing in foreign exchange terms, as they have made possible large-scale exports of coal and iron ore.

Another reason is that the country has been suffering from a shortage of foreign capital since early in 1976, and the authorities have begun to adjust their policies to adapt the economy to this new reality of capital shortage, which they sensed would be a permanent condition. For instance the large State-owned enterprises have started to move towards financing a higher proportion of their capital needs out of revenue. The Senior Deputy Governor of the Reserve Bank, Dr. Gerhard de Kock, said in a speech in late 1976 that South Africa had enjoyed a net capital inflow from abroad averaging 3 per cent of national output since the Second World War, but that this would have to be reduced to somewhere between 1 and 2 per cent.

As South Africans spend more each year on travelling abroad than foreign tourists bring into their country, a "visa war" could actually be advantageous financially if it made it more difficult for South Africans to travel abroad or settle in other countries.

If the U.S. opted for an "educational" campaign among the Blacks in South Africa to destabilize White authority, it would invite retaliation by Pretoria and lead to a shutdown of all American information-spreading and information-gathering activities in the country. This is already a sensitive point. In June 1977 the wellknown South African journalist Aida Parker, who has close connections with Government circles, published a whole series of articles in *The Citizen* newspaper, entitled "Secret U.S. War Against South Africa," in which she accused "agencies of the U.S. Government" of "actively trying to destabilize the position here by generous assistance to resistance movements, Black Consciousness bodies and would-be Black leaders."

She referred to "a massive and increasing flow of covert State Department-CIA funds," much of it funnelled through the U.S. Embassy in Botswana, a neighboring state that is politically independent of South Africa but is inside the South African exchange control system. She quoted the evidence of Harry Winston, a former chairman of the U.S. Communist Party, that the banned Black radical movement Pan African Congress was formed "in the luxurious offices of the USIS in Johannesburg." She accused the CIA of giving "covert support" (without their knowledge) "to organizations such as the Black Peoples' Convention, the S.A. Students Organization, the Soweto Students' Representative Council, the Black Community Program, the Union of Black Journalists, the Black Allied Workers' Union and the National Youth Organization—all legal bodies, but regarded by the South African Government as centers of Black radicalism.

49

She alleges that "there is scarcely a political trial in the country in which the CIA is not somehow involved" in financing of defendants, pointing out that among the members of the Board of Trustees of the American Lawyers' Committee for Civil Rights Under Law, which operates in South Africa through its Africa Legal Assistance Project, are partners in a law firm which was exposed in the U.S. as long ago as 1967 as being "engaged in funnelling CIA funds into selected targets." She reported that "there is evidence that several major U.S. business houses with South African subsidiaries are used both as covers and channels for anti-South African political activity and as fronts for intelligence operations." She produced evidence that "the U.S. Administration deliberately uses private organizations, foundations and institutes as a 'cover' for providing educational grants, some of which are used to benefit existing or potential members of so-called 'liberation' groups."

As she commented: "Over the past 3 years, in an attempt to slow or stop the rapid erosion of goodwill between Pretoria and Washington, Pretoria has found it expedient to tolerate gross interference in its domestic affairs, at an every-increasing rate, by various U.S. agencies." The reasonable inference from this remark is that Pretoria is unlikely to tolerate such interference for much longer.

This remarkable attack on the U.S. Administration by a source close to Government thinking shows the extent to which relations between the U.S. and South Africa have already deteriorated, and the degree of hostility toward Washington that is building up in Pretoria.

6.

Enemies and friends

President Carter should be fairly free to pursue a policy of escalating hostility toward South Africa, if he chooses, because the Republic has a limited number of committed friends and increasingly active and influential enemies within the U.S., while the great mass of ordinary Americans are indifferent.

The anti-South African lobby grows stronger by the day. Its numbers range from the most decent kind of humanists who want to do what they believe is morally right, to Marxist revolutionaries. The latter see South Africa as the epitome of everything they loathe. It is conservative, capitalist and racist. They claim elements of colonialism (Whites in a Black continent), fascism (police brutality, pass laws), exploitation (the White/Black pay gap, cheap labor).

This lobby draws its strength from several different politically influential groups. There are the political activists; Black groups and White liberals. There are the churches; missionary-spirited militants who are more concerned with social relevance than the life of the spirit. There are the academics; both students and their tutors in search of a "clean" and clear-cut new cause to follow their victory over the Vietnam war.

South African lobbyist Donald E. deKieffer puts the Republic's critics in 3 distinct groups:

- Sincere and partially-informed critics who base their criticism on their partial knowledge. "Worry about these the least," he says, "as we can enter into dialogue with all genuine critics who are willing to listen."
- Ignorant critics. One proof of the ignorance of ordinary Americans about South Africa is that a survey a couple of years ago showed that only 4 per cent of Americans could identify 2 or more cities in the Republic.
- The "professional anti-South Africans." These people embrace all kinds of causes, for instance pro-Cuba, anti-Chile, pro-abortion, anti-capital punishment. Although small in number, they are vociferous, they compose most of the anti-South African resolutions put before corporate, church and local government meetings, "they are the danger." And they aren't willing to listen to any facts that undermine the premises on which their opinions are based.

The anti-South African lobby is rich. The churches alone are estimated to spend at least $5-million a year on anti-South African activities. This is several times as much as the South African Government spends on its entire information dissemination activities in the U.S. Then there are the academic institutions that specialize in Southern African affairs, drawing their funds from several rich liberal (sometimes even radical) foundations. If Miss Parker is correct, there is also the CIA, using innocuous channels to "launder" its money.

The churches and radical groups are mounting an escalating campaign to pressure corporations into using their South African subsidiaries to change South African society, to cease investing new money in the Republic, or even to disengage entirely. They propose stockholder resolutions at corporate annual meetings along these lines, use the meeting to pillory company executives with long speeches accusing them of supporting apartheid, and bombard corporate headquarters with critical letters and telephone calls.

The institutions and radical groups also try to influence public opinion through their own publications, placing anti-South African material in the media, and talking to journalists. Activists are planning to destroy the remaining sporting links between the U.S. and South Africa by disrupting meets to which South African sportsmen are invited.

Student groups at several universities have held demonstrations to pressure councils of regents into selling the shares of corporations with South African interests held in the trusts they control. "South Africa," says Prof. Robert A. Price, "is the perfect target for the students because it is both a morally pure case for political action—there are very few issues around that strike students as being so uncomplicated—and because there is a direct connection between the universities and South Africa, via college investments."

Institutions and groups of liberal lawyers (originally formed to act on civil rights within the U.S.) are also bringing suits before the courts to increase the pressure on South Africa. For instance action has been taken against the *New York Times* to prevent it from accepting advertisements about employment opportunities in the Republic on the grounds that such advertisements are inherently discriminatory in favor of Whites, and therefore violate U.S. civil rights legislation. Another example is a suit to prohibit South African Airways from landing in the U.S. on similar grounds.

A recent development is the lobbying of city councils to pass resolutions prohibiting purchases from corporations with South African involvements.

There are probably only about 500 hardcore activists involved in the "African liberation movement" right across the U.S. But through more than 100 different anti-South African organizations, they can mobilize the support of many thousands of Americans, and can draw on the sympathy and financial contributions of millions more ... especially through church membership. Some of these organizations are linked, but most are independent of one another. However, they tend to cooperate in pressing individual anti-South African issues. Some are well financed, but most operate with volunteer labor.

The academic and liberal institutions include the American Committee on Africa, the International Defense & Aid Fund for South Africa, the Africa News Service, and a number of small bodies such as the Bay Area Namibia Action Group. Church and religious groups include the World Council of Churches, the National Council of Churches, the Interfaith Center on Corporate Responsibility and Episcopal Churchmen for South Africa. The movement's financial sources include the Ford Foundation, the Carnegie

53

Foundation and The Africa Fund. Sectarian organizations involved include the Liberation Support Movement, the National Anti-Imperialist Movement in Solidarity with African Liberation and the National Student Coalition Against Racism. Black American groups include the Africa Information Service, the African Activist Association, and even a Congress of Afrikan (sic) People. Support groups include the Lawyers' Committee for Civil Rights Under Law/Africa Project, the Center for Constitutional Rights, the Council on Economic Priorities, the Institute for Policy Studies and the Investor Responsibility Research Center.

Among the most powerful of these is the American Committee on Africa, which also controls or influences several other organizations. It has about 20 000 members including such prominent Americans as ex-Congresswoman Bella Abzug, labor leader Victor Reuther, actor Sidney Poitier and writer James Baldwin. It maintains a lobbying office in Washington that has worked for repeal of the Byrd Amendment (which allowed Rhodesian chrome imports into the U.S. in violation of a U.N. resolution), to prevent a sugar import allocation for South Africa, and to stop imports of Namibian seal skins. It opposed U.S. intervention in Angola, has supported boycotts of American corporations with South African interests, and tried to stop The Southern Co. from importing South African coal. It is behind a prestigious quarterly called *Africa Today* and a slick, popular-appeal bimonthly called *Southern Africa*. Recently it sponsored an "Apartheid Kills" poster design competition with a $5,000 first prize to "dramatically awaken people to the murder, injustice and oppression which is apartheid." It is also involved with a campaign to discourage people from buying Kruger rand gold coins—extensively advertised in the U.S.—on the grounds that buying Kruger rands amounts to "investing in oppression." Both directly and via associated organizations, the ACOA is believed to be spending at least $250,000 a year on its anti-South African activities, and expenditure is believed to be mounting rapidly.

The largest, wealthiest and most active anti-South African group, however, is the National Council of Churches and its member-churches, whose leaders enjoy enormous prestige and influence in political and business circles because of their status as fonts of moral wisdom. The NCC has 30 member-churches, and among those most active against South Africa are such important groups as the United Methodist Church, the United Presbyterian Church, the United

Church of Christ, the Episcopal Church and the Church of Christ (Disciples of Christ). It funds the Interfaith Center on Corporate Responsibility, whose Executive Director, Tim Smith, is the most active organizer of stockholder resolutions criticizing corporate involvement in South Africa. A number of the NCC's leaders are actually Marxist in their sympathies, because they consider that Communism is closer to the principles of Christianity than capitalism. Ironically, most of the ordinary members of churches involved in the anti-South African campaign would probably be philosophically and politically opposed to such activities if they realized what was behind them, but happily contribute to funds that they think go to help the poor or feed the hungry. One church organization, the Interreligious Foundation for Community Organization, openly supports and finances terrorist movements in Africa—it received $457,000 from various sources in 1975.

South Africa has little with which to defend itself against such powerful enemies. The Department of Foreign Affairs has an embassy in Washington and consulates in several major U.S. cities, and the Department of Information also has offices in Washington DC, New York, Los Angeles and San Francisco. But the officials who staff these, while among the country's best, are too few and have too little money to make a real impact on the American public. South Africa employs 3 lobbyists in Washington, including the brilliant young lawyer Donald E. deKieffer (who is generally credited with bringing about Congress's banning of cyclamates). And it also uses a New York firm of public relations consultants, Sydney Baron & Co, whose vice-president for international affairs, Andrew T. Hatcher, is a Black American who was President Kennedy's assistant Press secretary. But this representation, while impressive in quality, cannot compare in magnitude with the scale of operations mounted by countries like Israel, Japan, Taiwan, Iran and South Korea.

South Africa has no natural lobby within the U.S. to neutralize its enemies' power and to promote its national interests, as do countries like Israel, Italy and Greece, with millions of "ethnic" Americans wielding real political influence on their behalf. Some liberals argue that South Africa has enjoyed the support of one of the country's most powerful lobbies, the military-industrial establishment, but I can find little evidence of this.

Many military men appreciate the Republic's strategic significance to the West. But this is not a "gut" issue that would bring into play the political leverage of the military establishment as a whole. It cannot compare in importance with matters such as the development of technologically-advanced air and naval equipment for the United States' direct defense against the Soviet Union. Yet even on issues like this the military lobby has lost out time and again to the liberal politicians.

Many of America's large corporations have profitable interests in or with South Africa. But in no case are these so important in proportion to their worldwide interests that they are likely to use up their "credits" with Washington politicians to torpedo a policy more hostile to South Africa. Business lobbies are sometimes very effective when significant dollar amounts are involved. But on "social responsibility" issues (and South Africa is regarded as being in this category), the corporations are mostly like putty in the hands of the politicians and the bureaucrats. They are so much under attack on these issues that their whole posture is defensive and apologetic. Corporations with plants and mines in South Africa would probably fight (without necessarily winning) if they were faced with being forced to actually disinvest in a way that would cost them large sums. Probably not under any other circumstances.

The closest thing that South Africa has to a natural lobby within the U.S. are the organized conservative groups. These sympathize with African Whites for a variety of reasons—anti-Communism, perception of U.S. national interest, support for a free enterprise society, identification with a people similar to Americans, or simple racism. But in recent years South Africa has consciously neglected these groups. One reason for this has been the assumption that it is not necessary to expend scarce resources on cultivating them, as the conservatives are already on South Africa's side. Another reason has been fear of South Africa's automatically being associated with radical Rightwing causes such as anti-Semitism or extreme anti-Communism. Effort has been concentrated on middle-of-the-roaders. The flaw in this approach has been that these are almost by definition unlikely to come out in public as active lobbyists for South Africa when it comes to the crunch.

Among the most powerful of South Africa's friends is The American Legion, a moderately conservative ex-servicemen's organization with 4-million members. Its national executive agreed in May 1977 to promote "an urgent nationwide educational program on the increasing importance of the economic, political and military significance of the Republic of South Africa and the national interests of the U.S." Its national commander, William J. Rogers, has called for "a combined strategy that will link the policies of the U.S., NATO, friendly nations of the Far East and the Persian Gulf states with the policies of the Republic of South Africa."

As pressure mounts, South Africa could be forced to fall back on a more defensive public relations campaign, cultivating natural allies on the Right. But it is unlikely that the conservatives could be mobilized as an effective lobby unless the Administration moved toward really extreme measures. These would not only outrage the conservatives, but also give them a real chance to win support among middle-of-the-road Americans, producing a reaction in Congress and the White House, which are both sensitive to shifts in public opinion.

For the present, many conservatives are disenchanted with South Africa. They say that although its Government talks tough, its actions over Rhodesia, Namibia, Angola and urban riots belie that toughness. "The Afrikaner," one journalist suggested to me, "has gone soft."

Rhodesia is a particularly sensitive issue because the sort of Americans who naturally sympathize with South Africa sympathize even more with Rhodesia. They find its racial policy very much easier to understand and support than South Africa's Teutonic, highly ideological, complex and therefore baffling separate development approach. They admire the Rhodesians' gallant 12-year stand against most of the world, and the bravado of their military.

Many American conservatives believe that South Africa betrayed Rhodesia in the Kissinger-Vorster negotiations last year, and are consequently less sympathetic towards the Republic. They are confused by South Africa's support for majority rule in Rhodesia, and multiracial rule in South West Africa, while flatly rejecting these concepts for itself. Every time a South African diplomat reiterates publicly his country's disassociation from Rhodesia, this harms South Africa among its friends while failing to gain any ground among its critics (who are well aware that Rhodesia could not survive without South Africa's cooperation, and who don't understand the principle of non-interference in the domestic affairs of other countries, as the Republic is the only nation that actually tries to follow this highly moral principle).

As far as the vast majority of ordinary Americans are concerned, South Africa seems remote and unimportant. They are wrapped up in the social and economic problems of their own society, and they are more inward-looking, even isolationist, in the wake of the disastrous intervention in Vietnam. There is considerable sympathy for African Whites—but nothing more. The arguments advanced by South Africans and South Africa's American friends about the importance to the U.S. of the Republic's minerals and its strategic situation lack the vital ingredient of emotional appeal—without which it is impossible to mobilize broadbased public support.

Besides, several factors have effectively neutralized the possibility of such support. One is South Africans' habit of saying and doing things in ways that have done the maximum amount of harm to their country's international image. Another is the one-third of a century of unremitting ideological warfare against South Africa by academics and journalists. The resulting indoctrination has left many college-educated Americans with the impression that White Africans are racist imperialists little different morally from the Nazis, and has left many ordinary Americans with the idea that South Africans are a bunch of rednecks who at least partially deserve whatever comes to them. Most Americans have never met real live South Africans, and have little knowledge of the country.

Of course there is a potential lobby within the U.S. for South Africa that most people prefer not to think or talk about because of its embarrassing implications—the 88 per cent of Americans who are White, and who therefore have some racial sympathies lurking deep in the unconscious.

Dr. George W. Shepherd, Professor of International Relations at the University of Denver, has pointed out that racial linkages, one of the major determinants of U.S. relations with Southern Africa, are not confined to Blacks. He has referred to "the enormous racial, ethnic and ideological affinity between American Anglo-Saxons and the Anglo-Saxons and Afrikaners of South Africa."

"While Americans were not direct participants in settling Rhodesia and South Africa, the similarities of origin, conquest and development among settler groups have created a transnational White-dominated cultural system of great importance to American relations with these African areas.

"The force of Anglo-Saxon solidarity is still very potent in American society, and can be counted on to rally sentiment for a beleaguered Rhodesia or Whites under attack from revolutionaries and Communists."

This is a possibility that cannot be overlooked, but it has no practical relevance for South Africa.

It is unlikely that this potential could be transformed into real political clout on South Africa's behalf, except under the most extreme circumstances—such as direct Soviet or East German military intervention in Southern Africa, or a bloodbath in which the Whites are clearly on the losing side. Neither is likely to occur.

7.

How the U.S. gotten involved

On October 14, 1975, a South African armored strike force crossed into Angola at the secret request of the U.S. Administration to launch a whirlwind campaign that brought the tenfold stronger Communist forces there to the verge of defeat. Yet on December 19, 1975, the U.S. Senate, by a vote of 54 to 22, imposed a ban on all further American assistance, overt or covert, to the anti-Communists in Angola (who, notwithstanding the South African participation, were mainly Black). The South African forces and their Angolan allies of the UNITA and FNLA movements, poised to take Luanda and destroy the remaining Communist stronghold, suddenly found their American support withdrawn.

Unwilling to fight the entire Soviet bloc alone in such circumstances, the South Africans withdrew their troops the following month, leaving the way open for seizure of one of Africa's richest and strategically most important territories by Moscow's proxies—the MPLA, the Cubans and the East Germans. On March 31, 1976, the United Nations Security Council denounced South Africa (not Cuba) as the aggressor in Angola; the U.S. did not veto the resolution, though it knew that the allegation was unfounded.

This amazing and tragic course of events epitomizes the awkward and deteriorating relationship between the U.S. and South Africa. It is a relationship full of ironies and contradictions.

The Republic is one of a tiny handful of American allies in Africa (a continent larger than North America), and the only one with a military potential to act as a proxy for the Pentagon should it be asked. Yet it has long been denied the right to purchase sophisticated U.S. weaponry that is supplied fairly freely, and often given, to most other countries—including even Communist ones like Yugoslavia.

Behind the scenes, and occasionally in front of them, there has been a considerable degree of practical cooperation between the U.S. and South Africa in the economic, political and even military areas. Yet Washington has never been willing to risk any public action that could be interpreted as official support for any Pretoria position, even when that position has been clearly a sensible one. It is now increasingly reluctant to shield South Africa against even the most extreme of the hostile measures proposed against it at the United Nations.

In the past, all this didn't matter very much. The whole subject was kept on the back burner, with the gas turned so far down that the flame hardly flickered. The United States maintained its traditional policy of benign neglect towards Africa. As one writer put it: "Washington ... pursued the goal of a minimum amount of trouble purchased with a minimum expenditure of time, money and energy."

Robert Good, an American diplomat who was ambassador in Zambia in the mid-Sixties, was only speaking partly in jest when he said that among the world's important continents, only Antarctica was less important than Africa. President Lyndon Johnson said that he kept confusing Nigeria and Algeria because they both ended in "geria." This did not indicate Johnson's ignorance about Africa; it was his crude yet lighthearted way of telling his staff not to bother him with African issues, as he considered them unimportant.

South Africa? Its traditional political, economic, military and emotional links were with Britain, and remained so even after 1961, when it became a republic and was in effect expelled from the British Commonwealth. Although there were and are many parallels between the history of Americans and South Africans, very little of that history has been shared, although it is worth recalling that Franklin D. Roosevelt's first political fundraising was in behalf of the Boers then battling British imperialism.

South Africans—including, ironically, Afrikaans-speaking South Africans who opposed British imperial influence over their country —have traditionally looked to London for leadership and support. When Robin Winks, Professor of History at Yale, visited the Republic in 1972, he commented: "The U.S. is the most under-reported country in the world in South Africa; I have never seen a Press which so consistently ignores domestic America."

All this has changed since April 25, 1974, when the Portuguese dictatorship was overthrown and its successors hastily abandoned the African colonies that Portugal had fought so long to hang on to. South Africa's first line of defense against Black Power pressures from the north had collapsed, destroyed not by action from without (Frelimo never posed an effective challenge to Portuguese authority), but from within—by Communist subversion of the White officer class in Portugal, especially at the universities.

As if this were not bad enough, it was followed a year later by the conquest of South Vietnam by Communist forces, humiliating the United States internationally even as its people breathed a collective sigh of relief at home. This left the Soviet Union buoyed by success and free to divert its attention and resources to troublemaking elsewhere in the world. In the wake of the Portuguese collapse, Southern Africa offered enticing opportunities, and Moscow quickly escalated its involvement in the region.

For several good reasons, the Russians prefer to use proxies in areas far from the motherland. They realized that nowhere in Black Africa was there a proxy that had any hope against White Power, so they sensibly picked on the Cubans instead. Because of their partly African genetic origins, the Cubans are not so obviously alien in Africa (especially Portuguese Africa, where there are many mixed-blood people), as are Eastern Europeans. They are more "Third World" in their standards and outlooks. They have more missionary zeal than the ideologically-jaded functionaries from the Russian plains. And they can be ordered to take the kind of risks that Soviet forces cannot, because of implications for the detente relationship with the U.S.

Angola became a priority target because a Communist takeover was far less certain than in Mozambique, yet Angola was by far the more important of the two because of its strategic situation on the Atlantic coast and its natural resources. Cuba's Deputy Foreign Minister has admitted publicly that there were already 230 Cuban military instructors in Angola training MPLA forces in the spring of 1975—months before UNITA got its first South African instructors.

As the Communist wave has moved south over the past three years, taking Mozambique with ease, seizing Angola thanks to a combination of daring, grim determination and Western disunity, squeezing Rhodesia, threatening Namibia, frightening Zambia into collaboration and feinting into Zaire, South Africa has been thrown on the defensive.

There are many indications of this, for instance:

- The dramatic change in the whole thrust and direction of the South African Government's racial policies, the turning-point being its commitment to the Security Council on October 24, 1974, to "do everything in our power to move away from discrimination based on race or color."
- Prime Minister Vorster's detente initiative of 1974/75, which was an energetic attempt to establish working relationships with a wide range of Black African countries notwithstanding their strong opposition to apartheid.
- An apparent change of policy over Rhodesia from unequivocal but low-profile support to Kissinger-like maneuvering and time-buying. There has been the withdrawal of South African security forces and the switch to official support for the principle of majority rule there. There have also been persistent reports of armtwisting of Ian Smith's Government at appropriate times by means of temporary squeezes on lifelines such as ammunition and oil supplies and rail transportation capacity for Rhodesian exports (these reports have been officially denied by both parties).
- The more dramatic yet less disputable decision to grant independence to Namibia (South West Africa), and the strong encouragement given to the 107 000 Whites there (most of them South Africans) to throw in their lot with moderate and conservative leaders of the other races on a shared power basis, but with a steady retreat from the principles on which the South African handover was to be based.
- The almost panicky attempt to create an instant Black middle class by sharply raising pay scales, so the inflation-adjusted earnings of the average Black, Colored and Asian worker rose by almost 7 per cent a year over the 1974-76 period, while

those of the average White worker actually fell slightly.

- The rather careful and cautious way that the authorities handled the suppression of rioting in Black townships in 1976, compared with the traditional ironfisted approach of previous governments.
- The doubling in dollar terms of annual defense expenditure over the 3 years to 1977, to reach $2-billion (a leading economist, Dr. Chris van Wyk, General Manager of Senbank, has forecast a redoubling over the next 3 to 5 years).

Part of this pragmatic and flexible response to the Communist challenge in Southern Africa was a clear recognition by the South Africans that they had to try hard to improve their relations with the United States. The policy of largely ignoring the rest of the world was splended while South Africa was splendidly isolated from the impact of external pressure from Black Africa and from great power rivalry. The collapse of the Portuguese empire transformed the one situation and the Communist victory in Vietnam the other.

South Africans have a fond regard for the British and they are thankful to the French for selling them sophisticated weaponry over the years that other Western powers have refused. But they are realists. They recognize that the only real danger in Southern Africa is posed by Russian ambitions, and that the U.S. is the only real match for the Soviet Union militarily, economically and politically. "The United States," Mr. Vorster declared rather emotionally in 1976, "is the leader of the Western world, therefore it is also my leader."

But this did not mean that the South African Government was ever too hopeful about its prospects of achieving a significant degree of support from the U.S. Vorster warned his people in his 1977 New Year message that in the event of a Communist attack on the Republic "we would have to meet it on our own." Foreign Minister "Pik" Botha specifically rules out any hope of American troops landing in Africa to support the Republic, saying that the U.S. Army, because it is about 20 per cent Black, could not be ordered to fight against "Black brothers" anywhere in Africa without the risk of mutiny.

South Africans were also well aware that the last thing the U.S. would contemplate, after the divisive conflicts of the late Sixties and early Seventies over race and the Vietnam intervention, would be any kind of involvement in Southern Africa of American military forces—which would reopen both old wounds simultaneously.

Traditionally, the U.S. viewed Africa as almost entirely the responsibility of its Western European allies, particularly Britain and France, because of their strong connections with an intimate experience of the region. The only exceptions to this rule were Liberia (established by the repatriated descendants of American slaves), and more recently Libya and Ethiopia. Of these, only Liberia is in Black Africa.

The process of change in this attitude began in the Sixties as the U.S. started to recognize that the withdrawal of the old imperial powers from the continent, and their increasing inward-looking concern with the European Economic Community, was allowing a power vacuum to develop which both the Soviet Union and Communist China showed signs of moving into.

Yet the Americans continued to respect the strength and stability of indigenous White Power, as represented by South Africa, Rhodesia and a Portugal that insisted that its African colonies were integral provinces of a single Euro-African country, and seemed determined to defend that view to the bitter end. It was a strength and stability apparently not seriously threatened either by a countervailing Black Power or by Communist meddling.

Dr. Henry Kissinger, rationalizing his famous Second Option that became the basis of the Nixon Administration's policy toward South Africa, said "The Blacks cannot gain political rights through violence." This would "only lead to chaos and increased opportunities for the Communists." Constructive change "can come only by acquiescence of the Whites," therefore "we can by selective relaxation of our stance toward the White states and increased economic assistance to the Black states in the region, help to draw the two groups together."

The collapse of the Portuguese empire undermined the basic premise of this policy. Then followed the Angolan debacle, when political defeat for South Africa obliged its Government to abandon the sensational military victory it almost had within its grasp. A part of that defeat was the refusal of the Congress to "follow through" with the support privately promised by the Administration and the Pentagon. But another part of it was the refusal of a single Black African state — or even either of the Black political movements that South Africa aided in Angola — to express public support for the

South African intervention (despite private pleas for even greater assistance than Pretoria was willing to commit). This was a measure of the Republic's isolation in Africa.

The panic exodus of 700,000 Whites from Portuguese Africa who preferred flight to fight; South Africa's apparent defeat in Angola; the general acceptance, even among most Southern African Whites, of the inevitability of majority rule in Rhodesia and Namibia; defensive actions and changed attitudes on the part of a South Africa seemingly lacking self-confidence; these are all constituents of a new image of a loser the White African has gained overseas.

The loser's image is one that feeds on itself. Every change of policy is interpreted as concession, every precautionary measure as a panic reaction. Every setback for White Africans undermines their self-confidence, snowball-style, while reinforcing thinking among Black Africans (especially those who live in countries still run by Whites) that the sands of time are running out for White Power. Every sign of division among Whites, such as between South Africa and Rhodesia or among Afrikaners and Englikaners in South Africa, is seen by many Black Africans as evidence that the White man is behaving despicably, stabbing his own kind in the back, and defeat must follow inevitably from such ethnic disunity.

Lost causes are never popular, and especially so in Africa, whose peoples are especially sensitive to the realities of power and to the penalties of wrong-guessing those realities. Lost causes involving Whites in Africa are assured of particular international unpopularity. Lost causes aren't popular with the U.S., either, after the Vietnam experience.

Although it has never been spelled out, it seems clear that there was a drastic change in the U.S. policy toward South Africa during the Ford Administration's last year in office, in response to the new circumstances in the Southern African region as seen from Washington.

Till then, the less Washington heard about, was expected to think about, or was obliged to adopt a public position on, South Africa, the happier it was. What policy there was, was a low-profile one within the framework of Kissinger's Option Two, which specified a balanced and evenhanded (or fencesitting, some would say) approach to both White and Black states in Southern Africa.

The essentials of Kissinger's new policy seem to have been these:

- A much higher priority for Africa in U.S. foreign policy considerations, as the continent was clearly becoming an arena for superpower rivalry.
- A much tougher attitude towards White Africans to force them to bring about political and social changes that would make their region a less tempting target for Communist subversion.
- Careful phasing so as to make use of the regional power, South Africa, to bring about necessary change in the "soft targets" — Rhodesia and Namibia — before turning the heat on the "hard target"—South Africa itself.
- Attempts to bolster moderate Black African groups as the most attractive alternative, from the American viewpoint, to both White rule and the Black radical movements backed by the Soviet Union.

Kissinger had little chance to bring such a policy into flower, because it only seems to have evolved in the wake of the Angolan debacle in early 1976, and by the end of the year he was already a lame-duck Secretary of State. But in a round of whirlwind diplomacy in the summer and fall, he met Vorster for talks in Switzerland, Germany and South Africa.

The culmination of this activity was that the Rhodesian Government capitulated, abandoned its most cherished principle, and committed itself to a handover to Black rule within two years. The official story is that this happened because Smith saw the error of his ways and the impossibility of his position, and that South African pressure as different from advice played no part in this act of political suicide on behalf of his party and his people. This takes some believing.

On the other hand, why should South Africa go so far? The suggestion is that Vorster had no choice, that Kissinger threatened him with the same serious measures that the Carter Administration has been talking about—cutting off oil, a total ban on arms supplies from all Western countries, an offensive against the gold price, and removal of the United States' veto "shield" at the U.N. He also hinted at rewards for "good behavior" such as pro-South African pressure on the IMF, loans, a possible easing or even lifting of the arms embargo, and perhaps even recognition of the Transkei—the first Black homeland to be given its independence.

It should not be thought, however, that Kissinger's approach was totally negative towards White Africans, notwithstanding his threat to use punitive measures to obtain compliance with the objectives of his foreign policy ... measures far tougher than ever before contemplated against a country friendly toward the United States (or, indeed, even against a neutral).

Kissinger recognized in his National Security Council study back in 1969 that should there be escalating violence to bring about change in Southern Africa, there would be "Black guerilla and terrorist activity on a growing scale within these countries" and that "because of their support of Blacks, the Soviets and Chinese will become the major beneficiaries of the conflict."

As events turned out, the Communist Chinese were either unable or unwilling to capitalize on the collapse of the Portuguese empire, and it was the Russians who moved into the region. Kissinger recognized this threat to America's strategic interests, but could not see how this could be stemmed by White Africans alone. Their policies produced a univeral reaction of hostility among Black Africans which would make them fertile ground for Communist subversion. They also made it impossible, for domestic and international political reasons, for the United States to commit itself openly to their side.

Kissinger believed that the answer was to bolster moderate Black African groups as a counterforce to the Black Marxist movements, and to bring about a non-racial alliance between the moderate Blacks and White Africans—which could only be done by forcing the latter to make radical changes in their political and social policies. He recognized that this was a formidable task because of Black hostility to White governments, ethnic solidarity on both sides and White resistance to radical change—the last thing he wanted to see was mass flights of Whites from Rhodesia and Namibia similar to those from Angola and Mozambique, destroying their economies and the source of their military "muscle," and making them easy targets for Communism.

He demanded of South Africa that it help bring about a handover of power to Black moderates in Rhodesia and Namibia, calm the fears of Whites there so they would stay on under majority rule to ensure continued economic and military strength, and make some dramatic moves in the right direction in the Republic's own racial policies. If this were done, he held out the prospect of U.S.

military and economic assistance to bolster a Southern African alliance consisting of South Africa and a constellation of moderate Black countries, some of them with significant White minorities.

It is doubtful that there were any firm promises in this regard. After all, Kissinger and White Africans were aware both of the possibility that Kissinger wouldn't be Secretary of State much longer, and of the inability of any U.S. administration to commit Congress in foreign policy matters (South Africa learned that bitter lesson in Angola). But the feeling of the South African Government, at least, was that it had no choice but to go along with Kissinger and hope for the best. The danger of a refusal, with the Soviet bloc escalating its involvement in Southern Africa, was too great.

How this new and interesting relationship between South Africa and the U.S. would have developed, we shall never know. Jimmy Carter beat Gerry Ford and that was the end of Kissinger and his policies.

8.

Flawed logic of the new strategy

The United States' dominating foreign policy problem, whatever the Administration, is containment of the expansionist Soviet Union. This is a reality that no American President can ignore, not even Carter, with his obeisances to the liberals with phrases like "inordinate fear of Communism." And it should never be forgotten that Carter's tutor in foreign policy, now head of his National Security Council, is Professor Zbigniew Brzezinski ... a Catholic Polish refugee, and therefore almost by definition a hardline anti-Communist. American policies toward Africa, and toward South Africa, must be seen in the context of this dominating problem and how Washington believes it can best deal with it.

The United States' policy in the military sphere is inevitably defensive, as a war between the superpowers is unthinkable, and in the wake of the Vietnam disaster even limited war against Soviet proxies is politically impossible unless there is a direct challenge to a critical U.S. interest. (One Senator, when asked about possible U.S. military intervention in Africa, replied: "Africa? You must be joking. We might just do something if the Russians were about to take over Canada.")

Therefore, the Carter Administration argues, the U.S. must challenge the Soviet Union in the areas where it can be put on the defensive. Human rights is one such. As British journalist Joe Rogaly has put it: "We who live in the non-Communist world suffer from the disadvantage that our principles and beliefs are far more difficult to propagate than the simple faiths of Marxism and its successor sects. You cannot seek to set the youth of the world alight by describing the moral foundations of capitalism. But individual freedom, respect for human rights, and non-racialism, are all part of the set of ideals that, thankfully, young people can subscribe to." Their propagation also has the advantage of destabilizing the Soviet bloc by threatening Moscow's grip over its population and the peoples of Eastern Europe.

Another area is the Third World. Kissinger's view was that the U.S. had to concentrate its efforts on bringing about stable and harmonious relationships between the 5 great powers, and that the Third World was of secondary importance. Brzezinski's is that the stable Western and Communist blocs that emerged after the War are disintegrating, and that the Third World will become important in determining the shape and strength of the new alliances of nations that will merge from a reordering of the international system. Therefore the U.S. must bid actively for support in the Third World. The U.N. is an important arena for this bidding, with African nations accounting for one-third the membership.

The Carter Administration sees the United States' capacity to aid economic development as a weapon in its armory against Soviet influence in the Third World, because the Russians aren't good at this. Free enterprise as in countries like Taiwan, South Korea and Singapore, has shown itself to be far superior to Communism as a means of raising the living standards of poor countries. What's more, the Russians are a stingy lot, far less prepared to help the Third World with economic development. Over the period 1970-75, for instance, the U.S. provided $29-billion (1975 dollars) in official development assistance, France $12-billion, West Germany $9-billion and Japan $6-billion. The Soviet Union only gave $5-billion. While American assistance ran at a rate of 0.25 per cent of GNP, Russia's was at a rate of only 0.08 per cent.

However, the Administration is conscious that American aid has not been too successful in the past in the developing countries. That in fact handouts may merely line the pockets of already-wealthy ruling classes, and stimulate unsound forms of development such as prestige industries, excessive urbanization, and commodity-producing export industries too dependent on the vagaries of international trade. The Administration, as Donald G. Baker puts it, tends to "take a broader view of development, recognizing the fundamental need for changes within political and social sectors as well as the economic sector if development is to occur."

A third area of interest is the tendency toward fragmentation of once-monolithic Communism. The most obvious example of this is the hostility between the Soviet Union and Communist China, which the Nixon Administration exploited so dramatically. Another example is the growth of a "Eurocommunism" independent of Moscow's dictates. Washington is keen to foster this fragmentation by improving relations with regimes such as those of Havana and Hanoi.

Many flaws are apparent in the Carter Administration's logic. One is that ultimately a military threat can only be neutralized by a military defense capacity (wasn't it Stalin who, when being told about how influential the Roman Catholic Church was, asked: "And how many divisions has the Vatican?"). Real power in the world—economic, military, technological—is concentrated in the advanced countries of the First and Second Worlds. That's also where the food surpluses are. And that's also where most of the mineral resources are. The Third World would have no more than a nuisance value if the chips were down.

Besides, if the U.S. does want to cultivate the Third World, the emphasis on human rights, economic development and political and social reform seem unrealistic. The last thing that the Third World countries—the worst violators of human rights outside the Communist group—would like to see, are idealistic Americans stirring up trouble among their college students. Their ruling groups are also hardly likely to be sympathetic toward political and social reform subverting their power and personal prosperity. As for economic development, this is in fact not quite the priority that Third World leaders suggest, judging by their actions. Didn't India spend $600-million on developing an atom bomb, with 45 per cent of its people living below the official poverty line of $7 a month? The Russians are more cynical about these matters, and therefore more successful. They have found that guns for the generals and bribes in Swiss bank accounts for the politicians, and cultivation of those in power almost irrespective of their views or behavior, are cheaper and more effective ways of gaining influence in the Third World than economic development programs.

As for Communist mavericks—they may be suspicious of or even hostile to Moscow for sound nationalistic reasons, but they are a long way from being allies of the U.S. They are still ideologically committed to the downfall of Western society and the destruction of the values of freedom and democracy that are important to almost all Americans. When the chips are down, can it really be believed that Cuba or Vietnam would be more willing than Chile or South Korea to act in concert with the U.S.? There is also a fundamental conflict between a policy that, on human rights grounds, tries to link the U.S. more closely with, as Secretary Vance has put it, "nations whose views and actions are most congruent with ours," and Communist countries that are no less brutal toward their own people because of their differences with Moscow.

Certainly in Africa the Soviet Union has no doubts that expanding Marxist influence is to its direct advantage. Says the highly regarded, London-based, Institute for the Study of Conflict: "The objective is to create a cluster of Marxist client states fully responsive to Moscow's strategic dictates for further struggle against the West. But these strategic objectives are concealed and justified by Moscow under the all-embracing doctrine of the national liberation struggle."

If the U.S. is not prepared to counter the establishment of Marxist regimes in Africa on the facile grounds that they are really "African socialist" governments that will not advance Soviet interests, then it will encourage the process of subversion and overthrow of anti-Communist governments, Black as well as White. This undermines the United States' natural support base on the continent (unless of course Washington's Africa experts believe that Marxism is the wave of the future, and that Marxist states are likely to prove more appropriate allies for the U.S. than anti-Communist ones).

America's friends in Africa, Black as well as White, are distressed at the apparent unconcern of the U.S. (to judge by Congressional actions and White House statements) about the expanding Soviet bloc influence on their continent. This was epitomized by the remark by the U.N. Ambassador Andrew Young, publicly support-ed by President Carter, that the Cubans are a "stabilizing force" in Angola (which they are, of course—in the same way as a man with a jackboot on his neck is in a very stable relationship).

President Mobutu Sese Seko of Zaire was speaking for all of moderate and conservative Africa when he commented caustically: "Andrew Young says it does not matter if African states go Marxist because they will want to go on trading with America. Is that the position of the Carter Administration? If it is, we should be told about it and we will then be in a position to arrange for our own surrender on better terms today than tomorrow."

In similar vein King Hassan of Morocco has said that the U.S. does not appear to have an African policy, merely "a series of discordant voices from high officials." He went on: "You Americans conquered space but you are abandoning your place on earth. You no longer seem able to distinguish between friend and foe. We are not telling America to intervene, but to back your friends working in the interests of the Western world with assistance, economic and military, and diplomatic clout."

However, the flaws in the policy, and the growing antagonism of Black anti-Communists toward it, will not help South Africa much if President Carter is set on a confrontation. For South Africa is an almost ideal test case for the Administration's theories. It has become the international symbol of violation of human rights. It is the one issue on which the Third World is united (at least in public). Its industrial sophistication and natural resources, combined with the emergence of a large Black middle class denied economic and political power, provide the right conditions to check out the theory that political and social reform can lead to dramatic economic development. The argument in itself, by appealing to the greed of White businessmen, will divide and weaken White resistance to change. If the U.S. commits itself to the Black cause, it can pre-empt the Soviet Union, and could come out top dog when the White regime collapses.

It all sounds logical enough. But it is based on the shifting sands of a single unrealistic assumption—that the Republic will collapse within a relatively short period of time. Ironically, it is the liberals who mocked the "domino theory" that the whole of South East Asia would come under Communist influence if South Vietnam fell to Hanoi, who view Southern Africa in domino theory terms following the fall of Mozambique and Angola.

South Africa's critics have been predicting "revolution tomorrow" for 30 years and have been consistently wrong—there are few grounds for believing that they will be right this time. The California-based Institute for the Future recently asked a wide range of North American experts on South Africa if they thought there was a likelihood that White government there would be overthrown by Black revolution within the next 15 to 20 years. More than 90 per cent said no. This shows that there is a wide gap between the assessment of the Administration's policymakers and the experts (most of whom, incidentaly, tend to be on the Left of the political spectrum and hostile to South Africa).

If history is any guide to the national character of South African Whites, and to the character of the peoples from which they stem (the Dutch, British, Germans and French Huguenots), then it is surely more likely that outside pressure, and perhaps increasing internal problems, will strengthen their determination to resist, to dig in their heels ... to become another "Sparta," adopt a hedgehog posture, and ride out the storm. South Africa has the inherent psychological, economic and military strengths to do this if it so determines.

It is widely assumed in the U.S. that Black hostility toward African Whites is a sort of monolithic steamroller that will inevitably overwhelm the South African Government. Blacks are about as monolithic as Irish-Americans. Their revolutionary movements in Africa have always been, and still are, hopelessly divided by political factionalism, tribal loyalties and the personal ambitions of their leaders. By no means are they united even in desire to overthrow White authority. The most usual reaction of the African masses to calls for rebellion is apathy ... "a curse on both their houses" (White rulers and Black rebels), and a willingness to wait till it's clear who is going to be top dog. A substantial minority of Blacks will stand by White authority, work for it, fight for it, even die for it—the Rhodesian Government's armed forces, two-thirds Black, are proof enough of that.

Besides, successful revolution in any country, in any society, at any period of history, has required certain things. One is deep infiltration of the power structure by revolutionaries (impossible in South Africa, where the power structure is almost entirely White). Another is a period of tyranny followed by a period of weak government, as in Russia and France (few would be prepared to argue that this is the situation in South Africa). A third is a relatively safe neighboring territory in which the rebels can organize, and from which they can attack (South Africa has made it plain that no neighboring territory will be safe from Israeli-type reprisal strikes should it contemplate such a role). A fourth is a spirit of defeatism in the ruling class, and acceptance of the inevitability of successful revolution against it (South African Whites are undoubtedly willing to make many compromises with their Blacks, but the vast majority of them will never accept Black rule—they are no more willing to accept this than Israel is ready to accept its conquest by the Arabs, and are prepared to go as far as the Israelis to defend their freedom).

Unfortunately, however, none of this reasoning will carry much weight with the present policymakers in Washington. They view South Africa in terms of a carefully structured pattern of thinking (or prejudices, if you prefer), and what they dismiss as self-serving South African propaganda is unlikely to influence them.

9.

U.S. interests in South Africa

The U.S. has fairly important political, business and strategic interests in Southern Africa. Escalation of violence in the region, or imposition of a degree of Soviet control, would be significantly more costly, damaging and disruptive for ordinary Americans and for the U.S. as a world power than the Communist victory in Vietnam. In the past, Washington could largely leave these interests to look after themselves. Now it can no longer do so.

Many of its political interests were clearly identified in Kissinger's lucid analysis for the National Security Council in 1969, and time has not changed the analysis significantly. "Racial repression by White minority regimes in Southern Africa has international political ramifications extending beyond the region itself," Kissinger wrote. "Politically conscious Blacks elsewhere in Africa and the world deeply resent the continuation of discrimination, identify with the repressed majorities in Southern Africa, and tend in varying degrees to see outside relationships with the White regimes as at least tacit acceptance of racism.

"Because of the multiracial character of our society and our own racial problems, other countries tend to see our relationship with

Southern Africa as reflections of domestic attitudes on race. If violence in the area escalates ... the U.S. would find it increasingly difficult, without sacrificing interests, to find a middle ground in the U.N. on questions of insurgent violence and counter-violence in the region, and to resist demands for more positive actions against the White regimes.

"Many others in the Nonwhite world tend to share this view in some measure. The Communist states have been quick to seize on this issue and to support Black aspirations. Thus our policy toward the White regimes of Southern Africa affects, though it may not necessarily govern, our standing with African and other states on issues in the United Nations and bilaterally."

The Carter Administration sees an additional, and perhaps overriding, political interest—the destruction of apartheid as evidence of American concern about human rights. As Prof. Donald G. Baker put it at a conference in Swaziland in July, 1977: "Unlike Kissinger, whose primary intent in resolving Southern African issues was to prevent a further intrusion of the Soviet Union in that area of the world, the Carter Administration motivation is basically that of seeing a termination of the racial injustices that characterize the situation in Rhodesia, Namibia and South Africa."

South African commentators have been quick to spot the weaknesses of the Carter approach. For instance Dr. John Poorter, one of the country's most sophisticated conservatives, wrote in his news magazine *To The Point:* "This new policy, with its emphasis on human rights, has immense superficial appeal but, like many a ripe apple, conceals the worm on the inside. Its chief defect is an ideal of egalitarianism that ignores social and cultural differences which have no parallel in Western societies, but which are the roots of the socio-political order in Africa. A transplant of Western systems to African states has already had disastrous rejection effects in most cases. There is every reason to believe that the same would be the case if the Carter formula of Western-style democracy (which exists in the American imagination but nowhere in Africa) were brought over to the big continent as if it were simply selling 10-million bottles of Coca-Cola. On such over-simplifications, on such bland ignorance of the real issues of Africa, rest the foundations of the new, much-vaunted Africa policy."

Many South Africans challenge the integrity of the Administration's motivation, on the grounds that the campaign against South

Africa is too selective to be based on genuine universal values, on the grounds that Americans are trying to assuage their guilty consciences for their terrible past of persecuting Blacks and Indians, or on the grounds that Carter wants to divert attention from still-continuing and potentially explosive racial problems within the U.S. All may be true, or partially true. But none of this is relevant, in the context of a U.S. campaign against South Africa.

What matters is that the President and his men see human rights as an *issue* which can be used as a sound ideological foundation on which to base resistance to Soviet imperialism, and to promote cooperation between the U.S. and the Third World. South Africa is a convenient pawn and its resources and stability can be sacrificed, if need be, in this international battle of the giants. In Carter's case, there is also his political debt toward Black Americans. Although sometimes exaggerated—Blacks usually vote heavily in favor of Democratic presidential candidates—this is undoubtedly a factor. And Black political power is growing within the U.S. as Blacks become better organized. Blacks are well represented in the House and they are influential in the election of many important Senators. Black Americans, are showing increasing interest in the situation of Black Africans under White rule (though not, unfortunately, in the situation of Black Africans under Black rule).

It is clearly an important interest of U.S. foreign policy that violence should not be allowed to escalate in Southern Africa for American domestic political reasons. If this happened, it would probably trigger off waves of sympathy among White as well as Black Americans for rival groups in Southern Africa. This could lead to the same sort of division as occurred over Vietnam, but with a far more intense emotional identification with both sides. Ambassador Young has said that a bad blow-up in Southern Africa would have an unfortunate impact on the social structure of America, "because racial tensions in the U.S. are always just below the surface." The Sunday Times of London has reported that Carter, above all, "is concerned about present South African policies leading to a bloody civil war, which would be brought by television into American living rooms, with the predictable effects of radicalizing American Blacks once again and generating unwelcome pressures on his Administration."

Britain also fears this implication, as the problems affecting its Black minority are worsening and the support for radical Right-wing groups like the National Front is growing.

However, it looks as if it will be difficult to avoid extension of the violence already present in Rhodesia and to a much lesser degree in Namibia. Not only because of the great complexity of Southern African racial problems, which do not lend themselves to easy solution, and the growing impatience of Blacks—but also because the Soviet Union is apparently determined to promote violence in the region to advance its own interests.

What are the United States' economic interests in Southern Africa? They are significant—if one considers not only direct interests but also indirect ones, the interests of America's principal allies.

South Africa is an important international market for sophisticated capital goods, components, processed materials and sub-assemblies from the advanced industrial nations. In fact it is the fifth largest outside North America and Europe (after Japan, Brazil, Australia and Iran). It is one of the few countries that consistently provides the U.S. with a favorable trade balance. In 1976 the U.S. sold $1.35-billion worth of goods to South Africa and became the country's biggest foreign supplier for the first time. The favorable balance ran to $423-million. The Republic is also an important market for Britain, West Germany and Japan.

Any trade sanctions against South Africa, any restraint of capital flows or measures against South African exports that undermined the country's import potential, any pressures that encourage the Republic to become autarkic, any economically disruptive action aimed at destabilizing South Africa by means of encouraging strikes, civil disorder or terrorist activity, would damage business prospects for a number of American, West European and Japanese industries.

The Administration's claims that Black Africa is economically more important to the U.S. than South Africa, and is growing faster, are somewhat misleading. The economies of Black Africa excluding Nigeria have not been growing significantly faster than the Republic's, nor has U.S. trade with them. The U.N. Economic Commission for Africa released a remarkably critical report in early 1977 which said, among other things, that independent Africa had fared worse than any other region of the world in combating under-development, and that 36 of its countries had failed to reach the U.N. development target since 1960. In 1975 South Africa accounted for almost half U.S. sales to sub-Saharan Africa, which totalled $2-billion, with Nigeria taking one-fourth and the rest of Black Africa little more than one-fourth. According to Secretary Vance, U.S. aid to Africa totalled $271-million in fiscal 1976 and this is projected to rise to $450-million in fiscal 1978. South Africa has never received any U.S. aid and does not want it.

Nigeria is an important exception to Black Africa's general backwardness, because its participation in the OPEC cartel and fast-rising oil production have produced enormous additional revenues. To a considerable degree this is a "oneshot" phenomenon flowing from a quintupling of the oil price, which is hardly likely to be repeated. America's fast-growing trade with Nigeria largely reflects increasing oil purchases, and this is as much of a disadvantage as an advantage to the U.S. It runs a heavy deficit on its trade with Nigeria, amounting to $4.2 billion in 1976. By contrast, the U.S. runs a consistent surplus on its trade with South Africa. So the increasing U.S. commercial involvement with Nigeria really represents the price of blackmail by OPEC, of which Nigeria is a leading member. If South Africa is tempted into OPEC-style cartels in marketing its minerals, this would also lead to increased two-way trade with the U.S.—but hardly to America's advantage. Nigerian oil is attractive to American buyers, but it is not irreplaceable. If Nigeria refused to supply, it would have to sell elsewhere, and the U.S. would buy elsewhere. Shuffling the cards like this would help no-one, and the Nigerians are intelligent enough to know it.

In any case it is fallacious to believe that American business interests in Black Africa would be promoted be reducing U.S. trade with South Africa. The French have long proved that it is possible to increase trade profitably with both Black and White Africa simultaneously.

U.S. Business has more than $1.6-billion invested in South Africa. How much more, nobody knows, because that $1.6-billion is based on book values that grossly understate the real value of the assets. These investments are highly profitable. Consequently they have been growing rapidly. U.S. direct investment in South Africa almost doubled between 1970 and 1976, while investment in the whole of the rest of Africa actually fell over the period from $2.6-billion to $2.4-billion.

In addition, Britain and West Germany have heavy and growing investments in South Africa. Kissinger wrote in 1969 that in Britain's case income from trade with and investment in South

Africa played a "key role" in the country's balance of payments. "The British," he said "have made it clear that they will take no action which would jeopardize their economic interest." Any U.S. action against South Africa that disrupted Europe's economic links with the country would upset not only Britain but also its EEC partners and damage the fragile pattern of international cooperation.

More important to the U.S. and its allies than export markets and investment income, in the longer term, is likely to be access to Southern Africa's resources. The Republic is, for instance, the world's sixth largest food exporter. If the Soviet Union could obtain permanent control over South Africa's grain, it would be completely independent of American sources. This would not only be bad news for American farmers—it would also mean the loss of one of the few levers that Washington has on Moscow.

The region's mineral wealth is immense. It includes almost all the world's reserves of chrome and platinum group metals outside the Soviet bloc, most of its reserves of gold, manganese, vanadium and fluorspar, and substantial resources of uranium, diamonds, nickel, phosphates, iron ore, coal, asbestos, lead, zinc, vermiculite, titanium and other important minerals.

Finally, there is the strategic importance of Southern Africa for the defense of the U.S. and its allies, particularly the Cape sea route around Southern Africa, which has been called the West's "jugular vein."

According to a recent statement by the Foreign Affairs Research Institute in London, England: "Should the Soviets ever be able to deny the West both the minerals of Southern Africa and the supply of oil round the Cape route, the economies of Western Europe, Japan and increasingly the United States itself, would be in danger of complete collapse."

Washington theorists argue that the overthrow of White Power in South Africa would not damage American economic and strategic interests because the U.S. would find it as easy, if not easier, to deal with the Black Power that succeeded it. The United States' admittedly limited experience in Africa provides no evidence of this. Corruption is endemic in Black Africa and practised on a huge scale, so that it is impossible for anyone to do business without it—this puts U.S. corporations at a crippling disadvantage in the wake of the Lockheed scandal and resulting "honest business" laws. Africanization policies are not only widespread, but carried to extremes, making it very difficult for American companies to operate in Black Africa, because they are obliged to hire incompetents who are nationals of the host country. There is always the threat of seizure of assets without compensation. What American businessmen would be prepared to argue that it is easier to deal with Nigeria than South Africa ... or even that Mozambique's President Samora Machel is an improvement on Portuguese Commander-in-Chief General Kaulza de Arriaga?

It is the Russians, not the Americans, who have made inroads in Africa since the continent emerged from colonial domination. The chaos, the bloodshed, the deterioration in administrative standards, the accession to power of leaders plainly unprepared for it ... these have been the fruits of withdrawal of White Power from Africa so far, and those who have benefited have not been the U.S. or other Western nations.

10.

The human rights issue

The inspiring element in the policies that Jimmy Carter brought to the presidency was his commitment to human rights as a foundation of the United States' foreign relations. It would, he said, be the "first plank" and a "fundamental tenet" of his foreign policy. In his inaugural speech he said: "Our commitment to human rights must be absolute. The powerful must not persecute the weak, and human dignity must be enhanced. Because we are free we can never be indifferent to the fate of freedom elsewhere. Our moral sense dictates a clean-cut preference for those societies which share with us an abiding respect for individual human rights."

Part of the reasoning behind this commitment is to be found in Carter's book, *Why Not The Best?*, in which he wrote: "A nation's domestic and foreign policies actions should be derived from the same standards of ethics, honesty and morality which are characteristic of the individual citizens of the nation. The people of this country are inherently unselfish, open, honest, decent, competent and compassionate." Another part of that reasoning, according to the State Department's Director of Policy Planning, Tony Lake, is that it is in the United States' national advantage to go with and indeed promote the 3 most powerful "animating forces" in the world—peace, human rights and economic development.

Not that President Carter's "new approach" is really new at all. It is a return to an old tradition in U.S. foreign policy, described by the distinguished American scholar George Kennan as the "legalistic-moralistic" tradition. Even at the time of America's independence John Adams (later to be President) declared that the U.S. would eventually govern the world and introduce the perfection of man. After the First World War, President Woodrow Wilson declared that America's principles were not those of a single continent, but of a liberated mankind. President Franklin Roosevelt, shortly before his death, foresaw a new structure of world order, based on the ideals of American democracy, being built on the ashes of the Second World War. President John F. Kennedy used the same ringing tone of idealism as Carter, speaking in his inaugural address of "taking up the torch of the first revolution, the American revolution for liberty and human rights."

It is understandable and commendable that a nation founded on the spirit of the Pilgrim Fathers, built largely by the descendants of settlers who fled from religious and political persecution, and governed according to the constitution containing an immutable Bill of Rights, should concern itself with individual freedom beyond its frontiers. Indeed, it was surely the way that Carter's born-again Southern Baptist spirit reminded ordinary Americans of the old and true values of the past that, in the uncertain wake of Watergate, attracted to this relatively unknown selfmade millionaire enough votes to put him into the presidency.

Not surprisingly, South African Whites, who have been steeped in religious and ethical influences remarkably similar to Americans' over the centuries, at first reacted favorably to Carter's human rights initiative. They were willing to acknowledge their sin. But they recognized and responded to the traditional moral values that President Carter espoused. While the Russians, the Brazilians and the South Koreans were enraged by the human rights initiative, one country, and only one country, that was being criticized, supported Carter's principles. South Africa. Information Minister Dr. Cornelius Mulder said that the intention to make human rights a pillar of U.S. foreign policy "is something that our Government welcomes—provided, of course, that the policy is to be an honest one, based on consistent standards applicable to all countries, irrespective of their governments' policies and irrespective of racial or other considerations." Deputy Secretary for Information "Les" de Villiers told a British audience: "We have welcomed President Carter's initiative. We know that if this concern is based on really fair comparisons, we will come up smelling of roses."

What are human rights? The basic documents are the Universal Declaration of Human Rights approved by the U.N. General Assembly in 1948, and the Covenant on Civil and Political Rights passed by the U.N. in 1966. South Africa has never ratified either document. Neither has the U.S. Curiously, the Soviet Union has signed both. Which would seem to be a clear indication that, in the human rights business, what nations do is very different from what they claim to do, and that those that do not make far-reaching public commitments may actually do far more about ensuring fundamental freedoms.

The Universal Declaration pledges signatories to observe "inalienable rights ... without distinction of any kind, such as race, color, sex, language, religion, political or other opinion, national or social origin, property, birth or other status. Furthermore, no distinction shall be made on the basis of the political, jurisdictional or international status of the country or territory to which a person belongs." Basic rights can be defined, in terms of this and other documents, as follows:

● The right to life, liberty and security of the person. No man shall be subjected to slavery, servitude, torture, cruel or degrading treatment, arbitrary arrest, detention or exile. All shall be equal before the law, with the right to a fair public trial before independent and impartial tribunals, without presumption of guilt. And all shall be free from arbitrary interference with privacy, family, correspondence.

● Freedom of thought, religion, of peaceful assembly and association, and of expression, including "freedom to hold opinions without interference and to seek, receive and impart information and ideas through any media and regardless of frontiers." All shall enjoy freedom of movement and residence within a country, the right to leave it without hindrance, and the right to return to one's own country.

● All shall have the right to own property and not to be deprived of it arbitrarily, and to marry without any limitation due to race, nationality or religion.

- Participation in the government of one's country is a basic right, with the will of the people to be the basis of authority, this will to be expressed through "periodic and genuine elections which shall be by universal and equal suffrage and shall be held by secret vote or equivalent free voting procedures."
- The right to "a standard of living adequate for the health and wellbeing" of self and family, and the right to social security in event of personal misfortune.
- The right to work, and to do so under just and favorable conditions, with fair wages including equal pay for equal work, safe and healthy working conditions, and reasonable hours. All should be free to form and join labor unions, to strike (within the limits of the law), to enjoy rest and leisure, and to have "periodic holidays with pay."
- Elementary education shall be free and compulsory, higher education shall be equally accessible to all on the basis of merit, and parents shall have the prior right to choose the kind of education given to their children.
- All peoples shall have the right of self-determination, to "freely determine their political status and freely pursue their economic, social and cultural development." Nationality is also a right, and one may not be deprived of it arbitrarily.

Now these are fine principles, like motherhood and God, and obviously no country could live up to them all, no matter how well-intentioned. The realistic approach you would expect from the international community would be identification, exposure and condemnation of the worst violators of these principles. And clearly you would expect the U.N. Human Rights Commission to be the logical body to carry out this task.

Unfortunately, however, almost three-fourths of the 32 nations making up the commission are themselves accused of violating the rights of their citizens—including those model states the Soviet Union (which invented "medical torture" in psychiatric hospitals that now holds at least 20,000 political prisoners), Uganda (up to 100,000 dead in six years of "massacre, torture, rape and even cannibalism," according to the International Commission of Jurists), and Cuba (more political prisoners than the whole of the rest of Latin America put together). So, not surprisingly, the U.N. Human

Rights Commission manages to avoid condemning countries like the Soviet Union, Uganda and Cuba, while castigating repeatedly what a U.S. official has called "the iron triangle"—Israel, South Africa and Chile.

Who else is monitoring human rights performance? The U.S. Administration has started to, in terms of the 1976 International Security Assistance and Arms Export Control Act. The Department of State's first report, submitted to the Senate's Committee on Foreign Relations in March 1977, was what caused the furore with certain of America's allies, especially those in Latin America. But unfortunately the report is confined to 82 countries that receive some form of U.S. security assistance—this excludes the Soviet bloc, and also South Africa. Even among these countries, *Time* magazine commented gloomily, "human rights seem to be alive and well in only 23, barely one-quarter of the total."

The British Foreign Office assesses human rights performance on a global basis, giving equal weight to 7 criteria: incidence of imprisonment without trial, use of torture, absence of slavery, independence of the judiciary, freedom of the Press and access to information, freedom to join labor unions, and freedom to leave the country. At the bottom of the league are nations like Uganda and Cambodia (asked what has happened to 1-million people who have disappeared since the end of the war there, Cambodia's head-of-state Khieu Samphan did not deny they had been slaughtered, merely commented: "It's incredible how concerned you Westerners are about war criminals"). Others at the bottom are Equatorial Guinea (two-thirds of the members of the country's first National Assembly of 1968 have been murdered) and the Central African Empire (whose self-proclaimed emperor, Jean-Bedel Bokassa, is known as the French-speaking version of Uganda's Idi Amin). But unfortunately the Foreign Office ratings have not been published in detail, so we don't know how South Africa is ranked.

The best sources of information on human rights performance is undoubtedly the New York-based institution Freedom House. Its credentials are impeccable. It was created to alert Americans to the menace of Nazism, it was one of the first organizations to campaign for the rights of Black Americans after the Second World War, and it was among the first to oppose McCarthyism.

Each year Freedom House reports on the state of political and civil liberty in 159 countries and 53 dependent territories around the world, according to its own universal standards. A sign of its integrity is that it recognizes and rates Transkei as an independent country, though the new republic has not been recognized diplomatically by any nation other than South Africa which gave birth to it.

The ranking that Freedom House gives South Africa in terms of human freedom astonishes and discomfits its critics. In its latest survey (completed toward the end of 1976), it produced rankings showing that 93 independent countries have human rights situations inferior to South Africa's, including every African country toward which the U.S. is favorably disposed (Liberia, Kenya, Nigeria, Zambia). Indeed, South Africa stands out in Africa for the degree to which it offers political and civil rights to its peoples. Only two countries on the African continent enjoy ratings higher than South Africa's (Botswana and Gambia), with two others have an equal rating (Egypt and Lesotho). But both Botswana and Gambia have small populations. So in fact, of the estimated 375-million people who live on the African continent outside South Africa, only 1-million enjoy human rights superior to South Africa's Black, Colored, Asian and White peoples.

The singling out of South Africa for criticism, therefore, brings into question the integrity of President Carter's stand on human rights. Both Carter and Vice-President Mondale are demanding majority rule in Southern Africa without explaining why they do not demand this throughout Africa—the only way of determining whether a government has majority support is by holding a free election with competing parties, and only a handful of African countries have ever done this. Information Minister Mulder has commented: "I can think of nothing that would make South African Whites more openminded about constitutional change and movement away from racially discriminatory practices than witnessing the application of the principles of humanitarian democracy to all of Africa's 400-million people. But I don't think that this is what the Western powers really have in mind. On the contrary, the Whites of Southern Africa are singled out to receive moral lectures from those whose own records in racial affairs give them little right to lecture anyone."

Vice-President Mondale wants South Africa to release its "political prisoners," but makes no mention of political prisoners elsewhere in Africa—Tanzania, for instance, has 3,000 of them, many times more than South Africa is even accused of holding.

Ambassador Young (who, the President stresses, has his full support) has accused South Africa and Rhodesia of "systematic oppression and death dealing." Yet he has made no public criticism of Mozambique, where according to reliable reports 100,000 people are being held without trial in concentration camps under the most squalid and brutal conditions. Indeed, he has praised the "pragmatism" of the Maputo Government. The best comment on these double standards was made by the California Institute of Technology's Africa expert, Professor Edwin S. Munger, in evidence to the Senate Foreign Relations Committee in 1976. "There is something deeply racist," he said, "in acting as though Black lives and Black civil liberties throughout the continent are not important; that it is not our concern if Africans oppress Africans for example in Uganda, or in Ruanda, where Hutu murdered hundreds of thousands of Tutsi in a genocide. American criticism of wrong in South Africa will have greater credibility and impact if our strictures are evenhanded and not based on race alone."

Is South Africa perhaps a special case, because its sin is racism, and this is somehow a worse violation of human rights than murder of political opponents? The Administration has never gone so far as to argue this. But then the singling out of South Africa is not the only inconsistency in the Administration's human rights policy. According to the Washington-based Center for International Policy, which monitors American aid and human rights efforts, nearly one-third of the $9-billion the World Bank expects to lend in fiscal 1979 will go to what it considers the 15 most repressive regimes. Yet there is no evidence that President Carter is using the United States' considerable influence over the World Bank to change this situation—indeed, he opposed a move by Congress to prevent U.S. funds being given to such countries via the World Bank.

His criticism of human rights violations by Latin American friends such as Brazil, Argentina and Chile, which has damaged U.S. relations with those countries, is in curious contrast with his cultivation of unfriendly Latin American countries such as Panama, which wants back the U.S.-owned Panama Canal, and Cuba, which according to *The Economist* has "more political prisoners per head of the population ... than any country on the continent except Uruguay."

These are not the only inconsistencies in the U.S. Administration's human rights policy as it is revealing itself. There is also a flaw in the logic. The Administration is keen on cultivating support in the Third World, and says it believes that an active human rights policy will help this. The evidence points to the opposite. Among the two dozen countries which rate highest in Freedom House's rankings on human freedom, only a handful are in the Third World, and all of them except Venezuela are tiny and unimportant nations. On the other hand, of the 56 countries where human rights are least, all are in the Third World, or are Communist, or both.

Africa, which is an important part of the Third World, and which the U.S. Administration now seems intent on cultivating, has the worst record of any continent on human rights, and its rulers have the most to fear from the destabilizing effects of any U.S. initiative in this sphere. At the 1977 summit meeting of the Organization of African Unity in Gabon, the continent's most notorious butcher, President Amin of Uganda, was welcomed with rapturous applause, far exceeding that of any of Africa's decent leaders. There was no discussion of human rights at all at the meeting. And *Newsweek* magazine subsequently quoted an African head of state as admitting privately that "among all 49 member states of the OAU, scarcely a handful gives so much as an occasional nod to the currently popular subject of human rights."

The cynical explanation of all these inconsistencies is that Carter seeks to use human rights as a tactical weapon. He can use it to put the Russians on the defensive, as its deployment in a propaganda offensive could threaten Moscow's grip on its own people and on subject populations in Eastern Europe. This could induce the Soviet Union to offer real concessions in fields such as disarmament, in exchange for a Carter commitment to mute human rights criticism. He can also use it as a means of applying pressure to certain internationally unpopular countries like South Africa that cannot or will not hit back and damage U.S. interests (as Saudi Arabia, for instance, would do, if the U.S. Administration began pointing out publicly how undemocratic is its system of government).

The human rights policy, therefore, is not really concerned with human rights at all. It is a political technique to advance United States national interests as the Administration sees those interests, and to make ordinary Americans, who don't delve into the inconsistencies, "feel good."

This, of course, does not excuse South African violations of human rights. In many respects the situation in the Republic does not measure up to the standards that South Africans themselves would like to be judged by. Some of these violations, such as the pass laws, are difficult to remove without violating other human rights. Others, like restrictions imposed on the activities of Black businessmen, are unnecessary and inexcusable. Action on this front is essential as part of the multi-faceted response that South Africa should prepare to meet American pressure.

11.

The business connection

Business is the strongest link between the U.S. and South Africa. This makes it the most obvious target for anti-South African groups within the U.S., the easiest means by which Washington can bring pressure to bear on Pretoria, and the single most important area for South African promotional activity within North America.

Almost 400 U.S. corporations, including most of the biggest names, have subsidiaries or associates in South Africa. In some cases, like General Electric, the involvement goes back to before the turn of the century. In others, like Kennecott, involvement began only recently. Another 6,000 American companies do business with the country on an agency basis. U.S. direct investment in South Africa runs to almost $2-billion and indirect (common stock, loans) to as much again.

This involvement has always been highly profitable, with after-tax returns on direct investment averaging in the 16 to 18 per cent range. Some have done much better. One multinational set an annual return of 33 per cent as its target when it first went into South Africa in the late Forties and has never failed to meet it every year since, boom or slump. Much of that profit, of course, has been plowed back into expanding the South African operation.

Yet the risk and the hassle to achieve such returns have been less than most places else. South Africa has never nationalized a private company, and isn't likely to. It does not discriminate against foreign corporations. It has no laws that oblige foreign businesses to employ South Africans. There are no visa problems about bringing in managers or technicians from the States or anywhere. With a couple of exceptions (such as banks), there is no pressure on foreign concerns to take in South African partners. There is no public or private hostility of any kind to foreign interests.

The Investor Responsibility Research Center of Washington DC couldn't have put it better when it reported in 1976: "To most U.S. companies, South Africa offers an attractive business opportunity. The country's investment terms are generous, all current income may be repatriated, and the Government offers numerous concessions to companies interested in establishing operations in Government-designated growth areas, including low-interest loans, preferential transportation rates, cash rebates and tax concessions. Moreover, managing directors of U.S. companies in South Africa say the risk of political instability or Government interference adversely affecting their business operations is small. In 1973, a study by the University of Delaware placed South Africa among the 10 countries offering the most favorable business opportunities ... A number of corporate representatives (interviewed by IRRC) volunteered the opinion that there was less evidence of non-legal payments to Government officials and less regulatory bureaucracy in South Africa than in almost any other country in the world."

American companies play an important role in the Republic's economy. For instance they control 40 per cent of the petroleum market through Caltex (owned 50/50 by Standard Oil of California and Texaco), Mobil and Exxon (Esso). Both Caltex and Mobil have refineries, Caltex having just spent $130-million to double capacity. Ford and General Motors hold one-third of the auto market, their assembly plants going back to the Twenties. (Chrysler sold out to a South African group in 1976, but is still a minority partner in the plant that puts together its Dodge Valiants). In the electronics and electrical fields there are companies such as IBM, General Electric, ITT, Xerox, Control Data, Sperry Rand, Burroughs and NCR. U.S. corporations are strong in consumer goods, through companies such as Gillette, Colgate-Palmolive, Coca-Cola, Bristol-Myers and Chesebrough-Pond's. American subsidiaries make tractors, drugs, construction machinery, mining equipment, building materials and metal products. Service companies like Hertz, Avis, American Express and First National City Bank of New York are also there.

U.S. mining companies were late to move in on South Africa's natural resources, leaving the first century of development to British and later South African enterprise. But their impact in this sphere in recent years has been impressive. Phelps Dodge discovered a rich new mineral complex in the North Western Cape province that has already spawned 2 giant mines with more in prospect. Kennecott and Gulf & Western, through a jointly-owned Canadian company, are investing with local partners close on $300-million to produce titanium, iron and zircon from a 700-million ton beach sand deposit in Zululand. Newmont Mining played a leading role in establishing Palabora, a large opencast copper mine that is one of the world's most profitable. As minority partners, American companies are now into platinum, chrome, manganese, coal.

It is only in recent years that these involvements have become a political issue. Anti-South African groups, particularly those associated with American churches, have been tabling stockholder resolutions at the annual meetings of corporations with South African operations, critical of their involvement. These have always been voted down overwhelmingly. But they have caused company managements increasing discomfort. College students in California and elsewhere have started demonstrating to force councils of regents to sell university trust fund shares in corporations with South African interests. This in turn has prompted increased questioning of company executives from trustees and others about their South African operations. Congressmen, Pressmen and researchers are also firing a mounting barrage of questions at corporate headquarters. A few companies have faced demonstrations outside their offices, or even strikes to prevent their buying South African materials. All this, in turn, has prompted a much greater interest by head offices in the operations of their South African subsidiaries ... and a good deal of thinking about whether they should sell up and get out, both to get the critics off their backs, and because they foresee that pressures on them will get worse.

Basically, companies face 3 lines of criticism. One is that they are profiting immorally from the apartheid system by exploiting cheap labor and failing to open up opportunities to their Black employees. Another is that they are failing to use their position of influence to destroy apartheid. The third is that their involvement in the South African economy, and in particular any new investment they make in it, underpins apartheid.

The first criticism is the one that the corporations have done the most to meet—perhaps because Black advancement is an area where they can take action to satisfy critics without confrontation with the South African authorities, perhaps because there are some guilty consciences about the way they have exploited South African Blacks, and perhaps because management feels more at home tackling problems of labor relations than it does getting involved in political arguments.

General Motors and Ford, for instance, abolished separate pay scales for different races at their Port Elizabeth plants and started to pour money into housing schemes and sports facilities for their Black and Colored workers. They provided clinics, subsidized meals, literacy courses and educational assistance. To their joy they found that such moves not only paid off with the folks back home, but also paid off in hard cash—they experienced much-improved productivity, lower absenteeism, lower labor turnover and improved product quality.

ITT got its subsidiary Standard Telephones & Cable (South Africa) to introduce special training programs for its Black workers, and by 1976 had raised its proportion of Black employees to over 50 per cent. STC offers after-hours technical education to Blacks in mathematics, applied science, engineering drawing and electronics. The company gives university scholarships to Blacks for further study in South Africa, the U.S. and Europe; it now provides free medical care and contributes towards a pension plan on the same basis as for Whites.

Pfizer says that its Pietermaritzburg plant and Johannesburg-based distribution organization follow the same policy that the company applies worldwide: "To provide equal opportunity for employment and promotion, as well as equal pay for equal work without distinction as to race, religion or color, to the extent permitted by law. Bonus, vacation, educational assistance, pension, sick pay, medical and death benefits are provided to all employees without any distinction."

American companies are even moving in areas previously regarded as too sensitive. For instance Bill Marshall Smith, chief executive of Caltex, tells me that at their new refinery they have integrated the sports club and other facilities without experiencing any difficulty with White employees. A company that Allegheny-Ludlum Industries has a large stake in is running courses to prepare Whites for the experience, unusual in South Africa, of working under Black managers. Blacks have been trained as supervisors by Goodyear, as keypunch operators by Colgate-Palmolive, as computer programmers by IBM and as quality controllers by Union Carbide.

Sometimes racial segregation has been broken down in subtle and amusing ways. For instance one company went about integrating its cafeteria by initially establishing separate Black and White areas divided by a flower box with a trellis and vines crawling up it. When the vines reached the ceiling, the trellis was removed. Then the company stopped watering the vines. When they died, they were removed. Finally, the flower box was quietly taken away. Another company established a clinic for its workers with separate Black and White areas divided by a panel that was largely glass. Then the glass was deliberately broken and left unrepaired. Then the broken glass was removed. When there was no negative reaction from Whites, the entire panel was taken away.

Workplace segregation resulted from several factors. Firstly, laws which separated the races, or were interpreted as doing so, such as those reserving certain jobs for Whites or Coloreds, preventing Blacks being placed in positions of authority over Whites, or providing for separate comfort, eating and recreational facilities. Secondly, traditions, often enforced by White labor unions and codified by their agreements with employers—for instance, no law prevented Blacks being indentured as apprentices, but union-controlled committees refused to do so. Another example would be the opposition of White customers to being served by Black salesmen or technicians, which made companies reluctant to employ Blacks in such positions. Thirdly, the poor quality of educational and industrial training facilities for Blacks compared with those for Whites, and non-industrial cultural backgrounds (rural, tribal), made it too costly for corporations to train Blacks for the better jobs. NCR, IBM and Control Data, for instance, are on record as estimating that it takes 2 to 3 times as long to train a Black for a job as a White.

The whole situation has started to change in recent years, however. Job reservation is being phased out. "In practice, because the Government has granted so many thousands of exemptions to allow Blacks to do White jobs, only about one in every 100 (White) jobs is racially reserved," the *Sunday Times* of Johannesburg has reported. Prime Minister Vorster gave a public assurance in the early Seventies that the Government would not prevent Blacks moving into skilled and therefore higher-paid jobs provided such changes were made in an orderly fashion and with the agreement of the labor unions involved. This has happened. Companies began moving Blacks into supervisory and even management jobs, over Whites, without any Government action to stop them (though one Cabinet Minister caused an uproar in July 1977 when he said that shops in White areas could not employ Black managers). Corporations found that they were able to "reinterpret" laws always thought to provide for workplace segregation, to mean that they weren't actually forced to.

To circumvent the problem of labor unions blocking the training of Blacks as skilled craftsmen, the Government launched a crash program to establish industrial schools where this could be done. So as not to tread on too many toes, it said that the qualified artisans were to be used in Black-primacy areas only. But this is really an ideological fiction. Blacks are now being trained as engineering, medical and water purification technicians, as automobile and general mechanics, and as wiremen, carpenters, radiographers, plumbers, sheet metal workers, tailors and bricklayers. In addition, the Government brought in tax rebates for corporations running their own in-service training programs for Black employees. These are so generous that such programs cost the companies almost nothing. In special development areas there is actually a bonus, in addition to the normal tax write-off, equivalent to the cost of such schemes.

Traditional opposition to workplace integration has also slackened considerably. Integration of such "sensitive" facilities as cafeterias, toilets and sports clubs has been achieved without a single riot or strike as a signal of White backlash. John Deere's Fred Gilchrist wrote to the IRRC: "My managers are basically Afrikaans-speaking South Africans who have accepted this 'mood for change' very readily, and most of the improvements in working conditions, benefits, wages and so forth of our Nonwhite personnel have been suggested and initiated by my South African management staff." Many American companies have also found that they can now use Blacks in "sensitive" jobs involving dealing with the White public, without experiencing opposition—for instance Blacks are being used to sell veterinary drugs to farmers, generally considered the most racially conservative group among South African Whites.

Although Black education still leaves a lot to be desired, there has been great improvement in recent years. For instance the number of Blacks receiving secondary education for the first time increased at an average rate of almost 30 per cent a year over the 1971-75 period. This means that the quality of young Blacks coming on to the labor market is improving rapidly.

In response to increasing pressure at home, a dozen large U.S. corporations got together in 1976 under the leadership of the Rev. Leon Sullivan, a Black who is on the board of General Motors and several other major companies, to draft guidelines for their South African subsidiaries on fair employment practises. The "Sullivan Covenant" had, at the time of writing, been adopted publicly by 33 corporations: Abbott Laboratories, American Cyanamid, Burroughs, Caltex, Caterpillar Tractor, Citicorp, Colgate-Palmolive, CPC International, Deere & Co, Donaldson Co, Eastman Kodak, Eli Lilly, Ford Motor, General Motors, Gillette, Goodyear, Heublein, Hoover, IBM, International Harvester, Masonite, 3M, Mobil, Nabisco, NCR, Otis Elevator, Pfizer, Phillips Petroleum, Rohm & Haas, Singer, Sperry Rand, Sterling Drug and Union Carbide.

The Sullivan Covenant's 6 points are:

- Non-segregation in eating, comfort and work facilities.
- Equal and fair employment practises for all employees.
- Equal pay for all employees doing equal or comparable work for the same period of time.
- Initiation and development of training programs that will prepare Blacks for supervisory, administrative, clerical and technical jobs.
- Increasing the numbers of Blacks in management and supervisory positions.
- Improving the quality of employees' lives outside the work environment in areas such as housing, transport, schooling, recreation and health.

The South African Government has welcomed these principles as a positive contribution to workers' welfare. It has long accused the business community of blaming the Government for Blacks' disadvantages, while doing too little itself. Businessmen in South Africa have always been free to raise to any level they wish, the pay of Black employees, and to offer fringe benefits such as educational facilities, housing, medical services, pensions and transportation.

Personally I regard the Sullivan principles as inadequate, as they are not tough enough on closing the income gap, they make no mention of how improved benefits are to be financed (if the cost is simply passed on through higher prices, rather than being paid for out of enhanced productivity, Blacks as a whole will gain nothing). And there is no commitment to invest more and thus create extra job opportunities for Blacks, Coloreds and Asians.

South Africa's critics in the U.S. will not be satisfied with the Sullivan Covenant either ... for different reasons. They want much more. They do not want principles that Pretoria will accept, but principles that will bring U.S. business into conflict with the South African Government. For instance the Investor Responsibility Research Center, in its 1976 report *Labor Practices of U.S. Corporations in South Africa*, suggested 3 standards. Only the first of these—equal conditions for all employees to the full extent allowed by South African law and custom—would be met by compliance with the Sullivan Covenant.

Its second standard was: Go beyond the minimum allowed by law, and offer additional programs to compensate Blacks for the discrimination they have faced in the past. As far as I know, no U.S. corporation has yet been willing to adopt this concept, a concept which is in keeping with American liberal thinking that Blacks are unable to compete with Whites on a basis of equality because they are still disadvantaged by the heritage of past deprivation. One does not have to accept this to support the idea of special programs to advance Blacks, Coloreds and Asians in South Africa. What's more, I cannot see Pretoria having any objection.

However, IRRC's third standard was: Go beyond both minimum and compensatory efforts involving the corporation's own workers, and press the South African Government, White labor unions and Whites in general, to change institutions or policies that effectively exclude Blacks from opportunities enjoyed by Whites. This principle is so arguable and so political that its application would invite confrontation with the South African Government. Caltex's Marshall Smith, for instance, commented to me: "We are not and cannot see ourselves becoming associated with any pressure group. We are a foreign-owned company, and we believe that the only correct way for us to operate is strictly according to the rules laid down by the host. We shall go to the limit of what we can do within those rules." It is unlikely that any other U.S. corporation feels differently.

No matter what corporations do to prove their socially responsible attitudes toward their Black workers in South Africa, they will not be answering the most radical demand that is being made of them—that they should disengage entirely from the South African economy. A number of arguments are advanced for such action. That it's immoral to profit from cheap labor. That foreign investment underpins apartheid by strengthening the South African economy. That disengagement would register moral revulsion, which is worthwhile in itself, irrespective of practical effects. That improving the material situation of Blacks is actually counter-productive, because it lessens the pressure on them to rise up and overthrow the White regime. And that investment in South Africa is a bad risk, because there's going to be a revolution.

All these points are easily answered. For instance, the average earnings of Black, Colored and Asian workers in South Africa are significantly higher than those in most Third World countries. Their average earnings per month in manufacturing in 1974 were $127, compared with $198 in the Soviet Union, $121 in Brazil, $58 in Ghana and $31 in India. It isn't even true that the Black/White income gap is proof of discrimination, as this gap is actually wider in independent Black countries with significant White communities.

If foreign investment underpins apartheid, why do apartheid's opponents plead for it? The *Washington Post,* whose liberal credentials are impeccable, said in November 1976: "What seems to us the dominating consideration in this question is that South Africa's Blacks so clearly want American (and all outside) trade and investment to continue." Senator Charles H. Percy, a liberal, said after a thorough investigation in 1976: "A ban on investment would aggravate the plight of the Black majority without offering these people any hope for constructive change. Thus, I do not believe the answer lies in negative economic pressure on South Africa. I believe that American investment can play a useful role in expanding the pie and in seeing that it is more fairly divided."

Taking business actions on grounds of moral revulsion sounds highminded, but is a most dangerous principle. It is a positive invitation by the corporation involved to all kinds of political pressure groups to give them hell till they heed their demands. It is surely more sensible to follow the policy spelled out for me in New York by the public affairs adviser of one of the world's largest companies: "We do not believe that we have the authority to make political decisions such as boycotting South Africa, or Israel, or the Soviet Union. It is up to the Administration and the Congress to make such decisions, and we shall obey them."

This is also the answer to the suggestion that U.S. corporations should follow any kind of policy designed to precipitate violent revolution within South Africa.

Assessment of political risk in South Africa must inevitably be highly subjective. And there is no doubt (ironically) that what most U.S. corporations with South African interests are worried about today is not apartheid but the prospect that the White Government might be replaced by an anti-business, incompetent and corrupt Black one. But, as I have already said, the assessment of North American experts on South Africa is that there is a less than 10 per cent chance of a Black take-over in the next 15 to 20 years. And if the Republic is such a bad risk, why does the University of Delaware, in its latest Business Environment Risk Index, put South Africa well ahead of all other African countries, and even European ones like Britain, as a good place to invest?

Nevertheless, South Africans should not fool themselves. The Republic is losing ground in U.S. boardrooms. Corporate executives don't like their annual meetings to be disrupted, often by respectable clergymen who infer that board members are almost in the war criminal category for aiding South African "racists". They don't want hassle with the Congress, the Administration and the media over South African interests that typically represent less than 1 per cent of total company assets, and a not significantly higher proportion of earnings.

The man with direct responsibility for one of the largest single American investments in the Republic said to me ominously: "We cannot go on indefinitely supporting the South African Government." Another executive in a similar position said: "Unless we see signs of radical change, it won't be the Administration, it will be U.S. business, that will have to consider economic sanctions." ITT has already sold out of, or sold control of, all its major interests in

South Africa in recent years. Phelps Dodge, rather than develop the mineral treasure-chest of the North Western Cape itself, opted to put in no money and to trade its mineral rights for a minority stake in a mine to be financed by others. Both companies deny political reasons for their disengagement.

Of course, we should not over-estimate the strength of our critics, either. They do include a number of crazies who fortunately bring the whole anti-South African cause into disrepute, like the group that accused companies of plotting with the South African Government to set up Nazi-type extermination camps! The bigger companies are set up to ward off all kinds of criticism on social responsibility issues, such as environmental damage, nuclear waste, community control over boards of directors and equal opportunity employment. Provided Washington doesn't turn on the heat, most of the corporations can be expected to hang in there. But to do it, they could do with more help from South Africa than they're getting currently.

12.

U.S. defense and South Africa

When the Suez Canal was closed by the 1967 Arab-Israeli War, to rotate ships of its Persian Gulf force the U.S. Navy had to send them around Southern Africa. A destroyer, for instance, would leave an East Coast base such as Norfolk or Charleston and sail via Recife (Brazil) and Monrovia (Liberia) to Luanda (Angola). "From that point it would begin the longest and most treacherous portion of its voyage—2 800 nautical miles around the Cape of Good Hope to Lourenço Marques in Mozambique," according to Walter F. Hahn and Alvin J. Cottrell, in their book *Soviet Shadow Over Africa*, published by the University of Miami's Center for Advanced International Studies.

"En route refueling added about two weeks to the transit time. Moreover, the long journey was dangerous for destroyers because by the time they reached Lourenço Marques they were well below 25 per cent fuel capacity—a low fuel level for a destroyer. Rough seas encountered while rounding the Cape could endanger the ship and crew, because a ship low on fuel is less stable than one fully fueled. In addition, rough seas greatly increase the hazards of refueling."

All this was quite unnecessary. The U.S. could have made use of excellent South African harbors at Walvis Bay, Cape Town, Port

Elizabeth, East London and Durban. Better still, it could have used the elaborate South African Navy base at Simonstown, near Cape Town, which has the biggest and best drydock facilities between Europe and Singapore (it is now being tripled in size to berth up to 50 warships).

The Americans did not because of a political decision in Washington to boycott South African ports as a demonstration of disapproval of apartheid. Another part of that decision is the ban on sale of U.S. warships to the Republic despite the fact that, according to the British strategist, Air Marshal Steward Menaul, the South African Navy is "the only counter in the whole of the South Atlantic to the build-up of Russian naval forces."

It is doubtful that refusal to use South African ports has brought any benefits to the U.S. in its relations with Black Africa. It has been a rather inconvenient, costly and even potentially dangerous maneuver in the past, and could be more so in the future. With control of Luanda and Lourenço Marques (renamed Maputo) now in the hands of pro-Russian regimes, there are no suitable harbors —other than South African ones—available to U.S. warships between the Western tip of Africa and the Indian Ocean islands of Mauritius and Reunion (the U.S. naval base at Diego Garcia and the Kenyan port of Mombasa both lie far to the north). The U.S., say Hahn and Cottrell, "is rapidly losing its access to key littoral facilities and bases along the routes around Southern Africa.

"To be sure, U.S. destroyers destined for homeporting in Bahrein" (Persian Gulf) "can now again transit the Suez Canal. Yet this transit would not be assured in a conflict or crisis situation. Moreover, American non-nuclear attack carriers of the 70,000-80,000 tons class, such as the *John F. Kennedy* and the *Forrestal,* cannot pass through the Canal and are thus required, together with their escorts, to round the Cape to join other U.S. surface vessels for meeting whatever contingencies might arise in the Indian Ocean area. They would need enroute replenishment via the stationing of resupply ships and oilers at certain calculated intervals along the way. This had to be done in some measure during the Vietnam war, when U.S. carriers were moved from the Mediterranean to South East Asia." It could have to be done again in the event of a crisis in East Africa, where the Soviet build-up threatens Kenya, one of the few remaining U.S. allies in Africa, or in the Persian Gulf area of the Middle East.

The Suez Canal could easily be closed, by military interdiction or on political grounds, in time of war. What's more it cannot take fully-loaded ships larger than 78,000 tons, whereas between 80 and 90 per cent of all vessels now being built exceed 200,000 tons.

Consequently the Cape sea route, now considered the most crowded shipping lane in the world, is of critical importance to the West. According to the New York Times, it's conservatively estimated that 70 per cent of the strategic raw materials imported by NATO nations ply these waters around Africa. This figure includes 90 per cent of Western Europe's oil and 25 per cent of its food supplies.

U.S. dependence on this sea route is also increasing. The British Conservative Political Center reported in 1973 that "already 20 per cent of U.S. oil requirements are routed via the Cape and this figure is expected to rise to 60 per cent by the 1980s." Braam Fischer, the late leader of South Africa's Communist Party, once said that he would exchange all the country's fabulously rich goldfields for Cape Point—the rocky promontory around which all sea traffic between the Atlantic and Indian oceans has to pass.

Some strategists argue that the Russian Navy could interdict the sea routes from the Mid East to the U.S., Western Europe and Japan in several areas, and the stormy seas off Southern Africa would be the least suitable. If this is so, it is difficult to understand why Moscow has been steadily expanding its force of warships, supply vessels and submarines in the oceans around Southern Africa in recent years. Air Marshal Menual says emphatically: "The Soviet Union is quite determined that it will dominate both the South Atlantic and the Indian Ocean, and up to now we in the West have just sat back and watched them do it."

Some strategists also argue that South Africa or indeed any other politically secure land-based facilities in the region are unnecessary, as the U.S. Navy, the world's only "bluewater navy," can operate completely independently, anywhere, with "afloat support" such as oilers. This is true. But in doing so it incurs higher costs, less flexibility, delays, higher risk, and lowered combat potential should major repairs be required. Besides, the Soviet Navy, being technologically inferior to the American, does require such land-based facilities. If the Russians continue to be denied facilities along almost 3,000 miles of coast from the Namibian/Angolan border to the South African/Mozambique frontier (there are no suitable offshore islands that could be developed as an alternative), this would place them at a significant disadvantage.

Another argument is that control of shipping lanes would hardly be relevant in event of a war with the Soviet Union, which would mean a nuclear exchange. But this ignores the possibility that Russia could squeeze the West's jugular—its oil lifeline around the Cape—in a confrontation short of war, in the same way that President Kennedy was able to impose a naval quarantine on Cuba at the time of the 1962 missile crisis.

It also ignores the immediate political advantage to the Soviet Union of "showing the flag" and advertising its military might to African countries. In Marxist jargon, the Russian Commander-in-Chief, Admiral Sergei Gorshkov, puts it this way: "The Soviet Navy is a powerful factor in the creation of favorable conditions for the building of socialism and communism."

There are indications that NATO is becoming increasingly conscious that the Soviet Union is outflanking the alliance by moving toward domination of Southern Africa and its surrounding waters. This lies beyond NATO's southern boundary, the Tropic of Cancer, yet is assuming greater strategic importance for the Western allies. In 1974 NATO carried out a military study of the security of sea transport around Southern Africa—the first time it had undertaken the security study outside its treaty-defined operational area.

The Supreme Commander of NATO forces, General Alexander Haig, said in May 1976 that the Soviet threat "has become global in character, and nothing short of a global response will suffice as an answer." There have been suggestions either that NATO should extend south of the Tropic of Cancer, or alternatively that specific countries with substantial navies and regional interests, such as the U.S., Britain and France, should establish a separate regional alliance with South Africa, and other local naval powers such as Australia and Iran in the Indian Ocean, Argentina and Brazil in the South Atlantic. But nothing has come of these suggestions because of the political complications and their prospects don't look promising.

In April 1976 a West German journalist, Nils v.d. Heyde, wrote in the *Deutsches Allgemeine Sonntagsblatt* that "NATO Headquarters in Brussels has ceased denying that the Alliance is looking for new bases in the south that would make NATO fleet calls to Buenos

Aires in the west and Cape Town to the east a regular occurrence. It is no longer out of the question that one day South Africa and South American countries with an Atlantic seaboard will join in NATO talks in Brussels."

South Africa already supplies NATO with vital intelligence about the region. From a large and sophisticated radio monitoring and radar surveillance base near Simonstown, the Republic watches movements of shipping and listens into Russian naval radio traffic over vast areas of the South Atlantic and Indian oceans.

U.S. strategy in the region is presently centered on the island of Diego Garcia, south of India, where the horseshoe-shaped harbor has been deepened, the airport extended, and a sophisticated communications facility established. This is about as far from the U.S. as it's possible to get. It's not speedily accessible, and it lacks many advantages that would be available in South Africa.

The Republic's importance in Western defense is not confined to the naval sector. Its advanced engineering and electronic industries provide a substantial repair, maintenance and supply potential for any highly mechanized military force needing to operate in the vast area stretching from mid-Atlantic to the eastern Indian Ocean, from the Mid East right down to the Antarctic. In the Second World War, South Africa was the arsenal and principal base for the Allied campaign in North Africa. Secretary Kissinger pointed out in his 1969 study that "there are major ship repair and logistic facilities in South Africa with a level of technical competence which cannot be duplicated elsewhere on the African continent."

There is also the air route factor. In the 1973 Mid East war, U.S. transports flying desperately needed weaponry to Israel were unable for political reasons to refuel anywhere in Europe or North Africa, but were able to use the Portuguese-controlled Azores in mid-Atlantic for this purpose. With the political change in Portugal, these is no certainty this facility would be available in event of another Arab-Israeli conflict. In that case, use of South African air bases would provide the shortest secure and friendly air route between the U.S. and the Mid East.

Part of the American nervousness about recognizing South Africa's strategic importance stems from fear that by so doing, the U.S. could eventually get involved in Southern Africa in the same way it did in Vietnam, almost without knowing it ... with the same disastrous results. That is one reason why in the Senate vote on

Angola in December 1975, many hawks joined with the doves to block U.S. involvement. But South Africa is not Vietnam. It is important that Americans should understand the difference.

For a start, there is no question of involvement of American troops—not even advisers. South Africa does not need either, and is never likely to. It can mobilize all the manpower it needs from its own population—not just Whites, but other races too. The Rhodesians have already proved the competence and loyalty of well-trained Black troops. In South Africa, Black, Colored and Asian units have been formed, and preparation of officer cadres from these groups has begun. Whites already provide, or could soon be trained to provide, the skills necessary to operate highly sophisticated modern weaponry such as jet fighters, so the "advisers" needed by so many countries today if they are to field effective military forces will never be needed by South Africa.

If there is a danger of involvement of American troops in Southern Africa, it is not for their use in favor of the Republic, but against it. Obviously this would have to be done stealthily, as the American public would be outraged if it came to hear of plans now being discussed. One eminent senior U.S. combat commander now retired has already been approached and asked if he would consider heading up a United Nations' "peacekeeping" force in Namibia. No secret was made of the fact that this apparently innocuous move—sending in an international force in collaboration with, or to take over from, the South African forces in Namibia—would really be a "foot in the door." It would get the U.S. militarily and physically involved in Southern Africa in a role that would inevitably lead to conflict, sooner or later, with the Republic. In the lengthy stages leading up to this, propaganda developed around conflict between the U.S.—backed U.N. force and South Africa would tend to alienate American public opinion and neutralize potential political support for South African Whites. This could prepare the ground for eventual use of American troops to crush South Africa, though initially the U.N. force would be used to crush Rhodesia, then to guard bases in Namibia, Botswana, Rhodesia and Mozambique from which Black guerilla forces could operate against South Africa.

This nightmare can never become a reality provided the American people insist that not a single American soldier participates in any U.N. force destined for Southern Africa. They should remember, as David S. Broder wrote in *The Washington Post:* "That we allowed Lyndon Johnson to justify the American intervention in Vietnam on the argument that we were bringing the concept of one man, one vote, to the Mekong Delta."

There are many other differences between South Africa and Vietnam. For instance, Vietnam had little strategic importance for the U.S., and its loss did only limited damage—it reduced international respect for America's power and authority, and consequently enhanced the power and authority of the Communist countries, particularly the Soviet Union, which was Hanoi's principal backer.

The Communist path to victory in Vietnam was a long and carefully-planned one stretching over more than a third of a century, and it only succeeded because of the particular circumstances of the early Seventies and the major errors made by the U.S. in fighting the war. For instance, North Vietnam was largely left as a sanctuary from which the Communists could organize their penetration into the South. The U.S. failed to learn the lesson of aerial warfare in the Second World War that even the most ferocious bombing cannot destroy a determined enemy, and this would obviously be truer in the case of a rice-and-carbine foe than one leaning heavily on technologically sophisticated weapons and supplies.

In Southern Africa the Communists have only just arrived on the scene. They have no political infrastructure in their main target country—South Africa—and they are not being allowed to develop one. The Communist Party is not permitted to operate legally, and efficient and largely Black security police regularly smash cells as they are formed. The cancer is not being allowed to take root.

In Vietnam the U.S. tried to fight a revolutionary war with a conventional military strategy. A number of Western experts warned that this would be catastrophic, and they were proved right. South Africa does not seem to be making the same mistake. Its armed forces have steeped themselves in the theory and practise of revolutionary war, and understood how the Communist threat can be met and defeated.

In Vietnam the U.S. had great difficulties with an ally with whom it had little in common. The Vietnamese had a totally different cultural background, language, standards and patterns of behavior, with all that meant in terms of absence of coordination and conflict over goals and tactics. White Africans are people about as close, culturally, to Americans as you will find outside North America.

In Vietnam the U.S. was fighting on the border of a major Communist power, with all that meant in terms of inhibiting military actions and ease of supply for the enemy. Southern Africa is geographically about as isolated from the Communist heartland as you can get, and internal communications within South Africa are far more sophisticated than in the countries to the north from which any attacks would have to be launched. The logistics are entirely in favor of the defenders.

In Vietnam the terrain was ideally suited to guerilla warfare, with jungle mountains and paddy fields offering cover to the lurking enemy. Although there was a great deal of guerilla-type fighting in South Africa in the Boer War, that was before the days of the airplane. Today the large open expanses that cover most of the country can be easily watched by aerial reconnaissance, and security forces can be airlifted to any part in a short time to deal with incursions.

In Vietnam almost all weaponry for the local forces had to be provided at the expense of the American taxpayer. This led to a great deal of waste, and it also meant that when Washington "cut off the water", Saigon collapsed. South Africa asks for no gifts. It is largely self-sufficient in arms, and only asks of the U.S. the freedom that a large number of other nations possess—to buy highly technological weaponry for defense against potential enemies that could be similarly equipped by the Soviet Union.

Vietnam is a single nation which was divided by politics yet always remained united by language and the cultural bonds of a history of civilization stretching back more than a thousand years. It was not too difficult for the Communists to subvert their fellow-countrymen, to proselytize them with class-war doctrines, to establish their sources of information and logistic support right inside the opposing forces. In South Africa the core of the defensive strength consists of a White ethnic group that is deeply opposed to Communism by conviction and way of life, that cannot be subverted or infiltrated to any significant degree. And the most powerful psychological force in all groups, Black as well as Whites, is ethnic nationalism—which the Communists have long recognized as the most formidable ideological defense against their internationalist, class-war doctrines.

The unpleasant reality for the U.S. and other Western countries is that South Africa is placed in a strategically important geographical position, is the only country both friendly to the West and possessing sophisticated facilities of military value within thousands of miles, controls certain resources of considerable strategic importance to the West, and is the dominant military power in the region. No amount of distaste for its policies can outweigh these practical factors.

As Hahn and Cottrell put it: "From the vantage point of a strategic planner—whether he sits in Washington, Moscow or in one of the capitals of Western Europe ... this fact (the strategic importance of the Republic) must be faced irrespective of the political, ideological and emotional issues that revolve around the domestic policies of the South African Government."

13.

Mineral treasure-chest

South Africa's mineral wealth has more strategic importance for the U.S. than any other single aspect of relations between the 2 countries. Firstly, because the U.S. and its allies already depend on South Africa for a significant proportion of supplies of several industrially and militarily important minerals. That dependence must increase, as the U.S. comes to rely more and more on imports to meet its needs, and as the limited reserves of suppliers that are alternatives to South Africa are exhausted. Secondly, because control of these resources by the Soviet Union or any government less friendly towards the United States would almost certainly lead to OPEC-type restraints on supply of certain critical minerals to force up prices to several times their current levels. And thirdly, because in any confrontation between the U.S. and the Soviet Union ... any repetition of the 1961 Cuban missile or the 1973 Yom Kippur War crises ... the Russians could in such circumstances blackmail the West by cutting off supplies of critical minerals, as they did at the outbreak of the Korean war.

South Africa, it has been said, will be the Saudi Arabia of the Eighties. What is meant by this is that Saudi Arabia, with a population of less than 9-million and an economy not much bigger than Czechoslovakia's, has the world's second largest foreign reserves and wields political and economic power out of all proportion to its size—all because of its immense deposits of low-cost oil and its dominating position as a supplier. This has constrained the United States to seek to remain friendly with Riyadh notwithstanding the strength of the Israel lobby in America, the economic devastation being wrought by the high oil prices set by Saudi-led OPEC, and the continuation of a political system that hardly measures up to U.S. standards in terms of democracy and human rights.

Thanks to geological freaks of nature, South Africa is a treasure-chest of minerals comparable in importance with Saudi Arabia's oil. It is almost as strong as the U.S. and the Soviet Union in terms of its non-fuel minerals, according to former senior CIA official Dr. Ray Cline—with a fraction of those countries' internal demand for minerals.

South Africa has immense deposits of precious and base minerals, which in several cases constitute most of the entire world's known reserves. It is perfectly set up to become a major industrial nation because it has substantial commercially viable deposits of almost every non-energy mineral required by modern industry.

Even in energy minerals, the Republic is well placed. Although no deposits of oil and no commercially viable deposits of natural gas have yet been found in the country or off its shores, there are large, low-cost deposits of the two other major sources of energy—coal and uranium. South Africa is very coal-orientated, and depends on imported petroleum for only one-fourth of total energy supplies. It is also highly experienced at producing both synthetic oil and synthetic natural gas from coal.

South Africa already ranks with the U.S., the Soviet Union, Canada and Australia as one of the great mining countries. In the Free World it easily ranks first as producer of platinum and associated rare metals (88 per cent of supply), gold (74 per cent), vanadium (58 per cent), chrome ore (47 per cent), beryl (48 per cent), manganese ore (41 per cent), diamonds (32 per cent) and antimony (31 per cent). It is also a major producer of vermiculite (31 per cent), asbestos (19 per cent) and uranium (13 per cent).

Production on this scale is a result, not only of the freaks of nature, but also of the development of a technologically and financially sophisticated mining industry which is able to exploit

114

deposits commercially even when they are extremely lowgrade. For instance ore has to be blasted out of hard rock deep underground at depths of up to three miles, and ground as fine as face powder, to yield an average of less than 10 grams of gold per tonne of rock (ten parts per million). Rock containing only $3\frac{1}{2}$ per cent phosphorus is upgraded by a South African-developed process to yield phosphate equal to the world's best, sold at the world's lowest price. Palabora, one of the world's most profitable copper mines, is producing 120,000 tons of metal a year from an ore grading only 0,6 per cent copper.

Increasingly, the Republic is producing not merely the crude ores, but upgraded and processed minerals from the ores, so they are ready for consumption in the developed countries without the need for intermediate processes that need expensive energy and cause problems with pollution-conscious environmental lobbies. For instance South Africa is about to become the largest producer of ferro-chrome (after Japan) and is a major producer of other alloys such as ferro-manganese and ferro-silicon. Two giant plants manufacture phosphoric acid, largely for export, from local phosphate. By an upgrading process, millions of tons of blend coking coal a year are produced from inferior coals for shipment to Japanese steel mills.

In the energy field South Africa has struck out on its own with coal and uranium developments of significance to the U.S. and other Western countries.

It has the largest pool of knowledge of oil-from-coal technology as a result of a quarter-century of operation of Sasol, the world's only major commercial plant, which produces gasoline and a wide range of petrochemical feedstocks and petroleum products from coal. Now a second Sasol is under construction, at a cost of more than $2-billion, which is forecast to provide between one-fourth and one-third of the nation's liquid fuel requirements when it comes on stream in the early Eighties. An even bigger project, Coalcom, to produce 12.7-million tons of liquid products a year from coal, is being planned by a consortium of State-controlled and privately-owned corporations.

South Africa has also developed a Helicon or "jet nozzle" uranium enrichment process quite different from the gaseous diffusion and centrifugal techniques used in the U.S. and other countries, which is expected to provide nuclear power station fuel one-third cheaper than conventional processes. An experimental production plant is now approaching completion and things are looking so favorable that the Republic's nuclear scientists are talking confidently of having a full-scale commercial plant operational by about 1986/87. Such a plant would cost over $2-billion and, according to some sources, would be able to supply one-fourth of the Free World's requirements of enriched uranium.

In the future, South Africa is destined to become much more important in world minerals than it already is, because it is relatively more important in reserves than it is in current production. The Bosveld Complex alone—one of four major minerals complexes in the country, and it doesn't even contain any workable gold deposits—is estimated to hold minerals worth more than $500-billion at prices current in May 1977. Although figures vary according to who makes the estimates, and their assumptions, the following are the approximate proportions of Free World reserves of major minerals found in South Africa:

Platinum and associated rare metals	70 to 100%
Chrome	65 to 90%[1]
Gold	70 to 75%
Vanadium	48 to 74%
Manganese	60 to 73%
Kyanite[2]	63%
Gem diamonds	60%
Titanium	50%
Fluorspar[3]	22 to 30%[5]
Asbestos	9 to 16%[6]
Antimony	14 to 15%
Nickel	10%[4]
Zinc	9%
Iron ore	8%[7]
Industrial diamonds	8%
Phosphates	8%[4]
Coal	5%
Copper	4%[1]
Lead	4%[4]

1. Almost all the rest is in neighboring Rhodesia
2. Used in the manufacture of high temperature-resisting porcelains and to toughen glass
3. Used as a flux in steel manufacture
4. Whole world
5. Including Namibia
6. 100% of the amosite and crocodolite varieties
7. Fe content of 60% and above

These figures don't even include recent discoveries of copper, lead, zinc and silver in the north-west of the Cape Province. The scale of these deposits is still being determined, but the South African Minister of Mines at the time, Dr. Piet Koornhof, said in August 1975 that nothing quite like them, in size and mineral value, had been found anywhere else in the world.

In addition to South Africa itself, there are other countries in Southern Africa whose mineral wealth is critically important to the West.

Namibia, for instance, which is likely to remain within the South African sphere of influence after it becomes independent in 1978, already has the world's largest uranium mine and some geologists believe that the world's most extensive uranium deposits will be proved there. It is a major supplier of germanium (an essential element in transistors) and diamonds. It also has substantial reserves of coal, zinc, lead, copper, tungsten and vanadium. This single territory, Russian observers have noted, has "enough resources to meet the needs of the continent."

Rhodesia (which hopefully will remain within the South African sphere of influence after majority rule, provided moderates win out against radicals in the race for power), has most of the world's reserves of high-grade metallurgical chrome. It also mines corundum (used mainly in grinding wheels), nickel, asbestos, copper, gold, tungsten, antimony, emeralds and lithium (used in aluminum smelting, lubricants, air conditioning equipment, batteries, synthetic rubber and ceramics). It has huge coal reserves, and platinum has also been discovered.

Zaire is America's major supplier of cobalt, an essential constituent of special alloys used in aircraft engines and in other militarily significant roles. It is also a major producer of copper, industrial diamonds, germanium and tantalum (used to make certain kinds of high-strength steels).

Zambia is a major producer of copper, cobalt and beryllium (used pure or in alloys by the aerospace, weapons and electrical industries). Botswana mines diamonds and nickel. Swaziland produces asbestos and iron ore.

Unlike the Soviet bloc, which is almost entirely self-sufficient in minerals, the advanced non-Communist nations all depend on imported natural resources. The U.S. is best situated, because of its agricultural production and the availability of indigenous low-grade ores or reasonable substitutes that could be exploited in an emergency. But even the U.S. is 50 per cent dependent on foreign sources for its major industrial raw materials under normal circumstances. America's major allies are far more exposed. OECD Europe, for instance, is estimated by Dr. William Schneider, an economist and defense analyst with the Hudson Institute, to be able 75 per cent dependent, without America's "emergency" resources of low-grade ores and substitutes. And a growing proportion of those resources, such as oil, is coming from the Soviet bloc itself. Japan is virtually 100 per cent dependent on imported resources. Western leaders are becoming conscious of the danger this situation poses. For instance, Sir Neil Cameron, new chief of Britain's defense staff, told NATO in 1977 that in future the alliance might "be obliged to wage peripheral wars to keep its share of the world's resources."

The Soviet Union is conscious of the West's increasing dependence, and its potential value as a lever. One Russian writer, for instance, has referred to how "the state of the economy of the industrialized capitalist countries is already becoming dependent on whether they can retain, and on what terms, access to the raw materials and energy resources in the sphere where they once held undivided sway." Other Russian writers have referred to trade in raw materials as "the weakest link in the system of capitalist international economic relations;" to the "sharply intensified" role of materials in the world economy; and to the "political character" of the problem of raw materials. The message is clear.

Southern Africa is a critical factor in this dependence. The U.S. to a limited extent, its Western European allies and Japan to a far greater extent, already rely on the region for certain minerals, and that dependence is increasing. For instance in 1973 the region produced almost all the non-Communist world's industrial diamonds, 87 per cent of its platinum and corundum, 78 per cent of its gold, 77 per cent of its cobalt and 61 per cent of gem diamonds. To an important extent, there is a degree of dependence for minerals such as chrome (58 per cent), beryl (56 per cent), vanadium (55 per cent) and germanium (52 per cent). The region also accounts for a significant proportion of non-Communist world supplies of major minerals such as manganese (32 per cent), copper (24 per cent) and asbestos (17 per cent), as well as lesser minerals such as antimony (32 per cent), vermiculite (31 per cent), tantalum and colombium (28 per cent), nickel (7 per cent) and tin (6 per cent).

118

Once again, the Russians are conscious of Africa's importance. In August 1976 their official newspaper *Izvestia* referred to the African continent as "a storehouse of cheap raw materials for the imperialist monopolies." E.A. Tarabrin, a leading Soviet Africanist, has pointed out the growing dependence of the U.S. and its allies on African raw materials and has forecast that the dependence will increase. *Pravda* in August 1976 pointed out that the U.S.'s "share of strategic raw materials imported from Africa amounts to 100 per cent of industrial diamonds; 58 per cent of uranium; 44 per cent of manganese, which is used in the steel smelting industry; 36 per cent of cobalt, essential for aircraft engines and high strength alloys; 33 per cent of its oil; and 23 per cent of its chromium, used in the manufacture of armor, aircraft engines and gun barrels." Hahn and Cottrell have written: "In the Soviet view the 'national liberation struggle' in Southern Africa is bound to have repercussions outside that region, with the particular potential of causing serious economic dislocation in the West."

U.S. strategist Alvin Cottrell believes that because "any direct assault on the Western democracies in Europe presents an extremely high risk of all-out nuclear war and the destruction of society at large, the Soviet Union and its close supporters (particularly Cuba in the African context) may very reasonably feel, therefore, that their ideological objectives can be achieved at far less risk by undermining the economic strength of the Western world through denying, or threatening to deny, it those key raw materials found in such abundance in Africa. Conceivably, the mere potential of the Soviet bloc to act really decisively against raw material supplies to the West, both at their points of origin in Africa and at sea, could become enough to sap the political confidence and morale of Western leaders when faced with some really critical East-West crisis. The result could be a succession of major reverses for the West, featuring at each stage further erosion of its economic ability and political will to withstand the next advance of Communist influence."

Dr. Wolfgang Ulbrich of the EEC's Center for Industrial Development has estimated that Soviet political control of Southern Africa could give Moscow control over 97 per cent of the world's chrome, 90 per cent of its platinum, 80 per cent of its gold, 79 per cent of its vanadium, 74 per cent of its manganese and 40 to 50 per cent of its uranium. Information Minister Mulder has pointed out that "if Moscow controlled our gold mines, it could launch a freely-convertible gold-backed rouble that would destroy the Free World's monetary system." And King Hassan of Morocco believes that Soviet strategy is "to encircle, weaken and neutralize Western Europe by controlling its sources of key minerals in Africa."

There are some influential Americans, like Ambassador Young, who suggest that U.S. dependence on Southern African minerals is no good reason to support pro-Western White governments there, as whoever controls these mineral-rich countries, even if they are Marxists, will have to sell the minerals. As the Soviet Union is an exporter rather than an importer of raw materials, the only markets are the existing ones in the U.S. and other non-Communist countries. What's more, the U.S. cannot be blackmailed over resources because of its stockpiles, which would allow time to exploit indigenous low-grade ores and/or develop substitutes.

This view is rather naive.

It completely ignores the extent to which Americans benefit financially from their mining companies' free access to Southern Africa's resources. They are able to move in and develop ore deposits in a favorable business environment free of the problems of anti-foreign sentiment, political instability, official corruption and nepotism, threatened nationalization, official interference, sudden restrictions on export, and sudden tax boosts, prevalent in most other mineral-rich countries outside North America. They could hardly expect a friendly welcome from a hardline Marxist regime like that of Samora Machel—or even from one like that of a socialist dictator such as Julius Nyerere.

It ignores the probability that new rulers would willingly collaborate with the Russians in OPEC-type cartels to hold the West to ransom for their financial advantage. And the reasonable possibility that they might, under pressure from Moscow, withhold supplies, even if only temporarily, to strengthen the Russians' bargaining position in any East-West confrontation.

According to Hahn and Cottrell, "Soviet leaders ... are keenly sensitive to the debilitations that even a temporary denial of strategic resources can wreak on Western economies. To be sure, the Western nations could find other suppliers or develop resources elsewhere. However, the recasting of trade ties would require time, as would the exploitation of new mineral reserves. Prices, moreover, would inevitably rise." The non-Communist economies "would suffer severely." Dr. Schneider says: "Denial of access to foreign resources would be likely to suspend economic growth in Western Europe and Japan for many years, pending a radical improvement in the technology for exploiting indigenous resources."

The Russians would seem to have four clear objectives in extending their degree of control over supplies of the trade in critical minerals:

● Firstly, as they are themselves major producers, and raw materials are the only things they can sell to the West on any scale to pay for essential imports of food and technologically-sophisticated capital goods, they stand to gain enormously from any producer cartels that push up prices by restricting supplies. That was why they promoted the OPEC cartel so enthusiastically, years before 1973.

● Secondly, there are political advantages to be gained from backing Third World producers of commodities in their arguments with Western industrialized countries for higher prices, and the more the Russians control minerals, the more they will be able to support and influence the Third World's efforts.

● Thirdly, the higher commodity prices can be pushed, the greater the damage to Western countries' industries, as OPEC's successes since 1973 have shown.

● Fourthly, control over strategic materials has a direct military value. 20 years ago a Russian expert in economic warfare, Major General A.N. Lagovskiy, identified what he called the "weak link" in the West's military strength. Manufacture of modern arms, he pointed out, depended on certain critical raw materials such as chrome, platinum, nickel, cobalt and titanium. He drew attention to the fact that in the case of chrome, for instance, the U.S. had almost no resources of its own, yet this mineral was essential for the production of alloys for jet engines, gas turbines, guns and armor piercing projectiles. General Lagovskiy said that the Soviet Union should plan to exploit this weakness.

Experts now calculate that the United States has to import 80 per cent of the minerals which Lagovskiy identified as weak links—those that are essential for high technology weapon systems, and even aircraft production. Several of these come largely or even almost exclusively from Southern Africa.

14.

U.S. dependence on South Africa

There are 20 non-fuel raw materials that are vitally important to U.S. national security and industrial production, according to a report in December 1974 by the Council on International Economic Policy. These are alumina, bauxite, chromium, cobalt, columbium, copper, fluorspar, iron ore, lead, manganese, mercury, natural rubber, nickel, phosphates, platinum group metals, tin, titanium, tungsten, vanadium and zinc. The U.S. is already totally or largely dependent on imports for 13 of these.

Southern Africa is already the major or an important supplier to the U.S. and its Western allies of 7 of these 20 critical minerals—chromium, cobalt, columbium/tantalite, copper, manganese, platinum group metals and vanadium. It is likely to become important as a supplier of 7 others, as a result of mining development now in hand—fluorspar, iron ore, lead, nickel, phosphates, titanium and zinc. Then there are the energy minerals, coal and uranium, which are also growing in importance.

The flow of minerals from South Africa alone, to the U.S. alone, is substantial and growing rapidly. Between 1971 and 1975 U.S. imports of South African minerals tripled. A U.S. Treasury official told a Congressional investigation in mid-1976: "There is no question that many of South Africa's minerals are important to our economy, and that alternative sources of supply for some are not readily available or are unavailable."

The U.S. and other major non-Communist nations are already significantly dependent on South Africa for supplies of 3 major minerals—chrome, platinum and manganese.

Chrome was the first mineral to be put on the United States' strategic stockpile list. Three-fourths of the chromium used in the United States is consumed by the metallurgical industry. Most of it goes into the manufacture of stainless steels, although it is also employed in making alloy steels such as tool steels, superalloys for jet engines and engines and chemical processing equipment, and cast iron. The balance is consumed in the manufacture of refractory bricks for metallurgical operations, and to make sodium dichromate, a chemical used in products for the electroplating, pigment, leather tanning and other industries.

Chrome is an essential constituent of stainless steels because of the very high corrosion resistance and high degree of heat resistance that it imparts. It also provides the well-known shiny look that leads to its use for cosmetic purposes, as on automobile trim. Between 200 and 500 lbs of chromium go into every ton of stainless produced (depending on the type).

"Chromite ore, notably the highest grade of metallurgical grade chromium, of which some 90 per cent of the known world resources are located in Southern Africa, is essential to the production of certain alloy steels and is not interchangeable with another element," say Hahn and Cottrell in *Soviet Shadow Over Africa*. "The only major substitute for Southern Africa as a source for chromium is the Soviet Union. Neither are there acceptable substitutes for platinum, or for metallurgical grade manganese. The demand for these minerals is unlikely to dwindle."

In a recent study for the U.S. Administration, Charles River Associates of Cambridge, Mass., concluded that it would be possible to economize on U.S. chrome consumption—running at about 540,000 tons a year in the mid-Seventies—by lowering the chromium content of many steels to the lowest present proportion (10 per cent), and by using substitute materials such as coated steels, aluminum, plastics and titanium, in many applications. Substitutes could replace stainless in uses such as automobile trim, food processing equipment and kitchenware, which account for about half of consumption. Though costly, they could also replace stainless in conditions where severe corrosion is not involved, as in many chemical industry applications—accounting for about one-third of consumption.

But one-sixth of stainless is needed for conditions of extreme temperature, stress or corrosion. "No substitutes are available to replace the chromium in most superalloys" used in specialized applications such as jet engines and chemical processing equipment. In the Second World War, when Germany was cut off from its chrome supplies from Turkey, Armaments Minister Albert Speer told Hitler that irrespective of what else the Allies did, the country's weapons industry would come to a halt in January, 1946 when the chromium stockpile would be exhausted—an indication of chrome's critical military importance.

The U.S. imports all its chrome, and what unmined resources it has are very low-grade and limited relative to consumption of the ore and its ferroalloys, though it does have a stockpile equivalent to 3 years' normal consumption. Charles River Associates concluded that the U.S. "is vulnerable to disruption of its foreign chromium supplies."

These figures show the major suppliers of U.S. chrome imports in 1974 by category of material:

Low carbon ferrochrome: South Africa 40%, Japan 16%, Rhodesia 11%.
High carbon ferrochrome: South Africa 38%, Rhodesia 25%.
Metallurgical grade chromite: Russia 51%, South Africa 17%, Turkey 17%, Rhodesia 13%
Chemical grade* chromite: South Africa 87%, Turkey 8%.
Refractory grade chromite: Philippines 79%, Russia 15%.

Reserves of countries outside Southern Africa are extremely limited. The Soviet Union is expected to have exhausted all its known reserves, both economic and sub-economic, by the year 2000. Turkey's deposits are forecast to be mined out in 10 to 20 years. The Philippines has only 5 to 6 years' reserves of high-grade ore at current rates of production. India has enough for 35 to 40 years at

---

*This grade is in fact being used increasingly to make stainless steel by the argon-oxygen-decarbonization process.

current rates but its metallurgical ores have undesirable characteristics, and mining methods and port facilities are said to be "inadequate to handle large output efficiently".

Charles River Associates concluded: "It seems probable that at some point in the future chromite production will become highly concentrated in Southern Africa, unless major new ore deposits are discovered elsewhere." And it referred to "South Africa's stated ambitions to increase greatly, in fact eventually to dominate, the world chromite and ferrochromium markets. All the indications are that they have the reserves of ore and the comparative advantage in efficiency of production to do so."

Chrome, it seems, is a much rarer and more valuable commodity than petroleum. High-grade chromite was priced at about $75 a ton in mid-1975, or roughly the same as the cartel-boosted price of crude oil. It's estimated that the price could soar to above $600 a ton in event of a 15 per cent fall-off of world supply, and to well over $1,000 in the case of a 26 per cent cutback. If world production were constrained by 26 per cent on a permanent basis, it would cost the U.S. more than $2-billion over a 15 year period. South Africa and the Soviet Union each supplied 26 per cent of the world's chromite in 1974, Rhodesia supplied 8 per cent. All were relatively more important if low-grade refractory chrome is excluded.

Compared with chrome, platinum and the other precious metals associated with it (palladium, rhodium, ruthenium, iridium and osmium) are more glamorous, and at first sight seem less strategically vital.

Platinum is about as valuable as gold. And like gold, its largest single use is in jewelry—especially in Japan, where the ladies consider it suits their skin color better than gold. About one-fourth the platinum marketed each year goes into jewelry. But these precious metals also have many specialized uses in industry, and in some of them they are virtually irreplaceable. The PGMs (platinum group metals) have unique catalytic properties—they promote chemical reactions without becoming part of the reactions. They have the greatest resistance to corrosion of any known metals. They have a very high melting point, and a remarkably high electrical conductivity.

In most modern oil refineries, platinum catalysts are essential both for platforming (improving the percentage of high quality gasolines produced) and for hydro-cracking (the most economical process for obtaining a high percentage of gasolines—as against other fractions like kerosenes—from crude oil). In chemical manufacture, platinum catalysts are the foundation of economical production of such essentials as petro-chemicals (for a whole galaxy of items from synthetic rubber to plastics to missile fuels) and nitric acid (for fertilizer production). In the electrical industries platinum has a wide range of uses in items such as contacts (especially for communications) and special fuses and resistors. In the glass industry platinum is found in feeder orifices for bottle, lens and fiberglass manufacture, and is coated on the concrete beam used to skim impurities off molten glass.

Platinum is an essential part of automobile exhaust anti-pollution systems—there is about one-twentieth of an ounce in each catalytic converter. It is used in sensitive instruments, especially those employed in high temperature furnaces. In laboratory equipment such as crucibles, forceps and combustion boats. In the linings of plutonium plants, where it resists fiercely corrosive gases and liquids. In the powerful miniature magnets used in hearing aids. In cathodic equipment to protect ships and oil pipelines. In the spinning jets that form nylon and rayon for clothes and tires. In air pollution equipment, dentists' amalgams and ceramics. All the time new uses are being found for this wonder metal—the latest is a revolutionary fuel cell now in production in America.

Not surprisingly, the U.S. is a big user of platinum, palladium and the lesser PGMs—more than 2-million ounces a year, at a cost of around a quarter-billion dollars. Auto anti-pollution devices alone require more than half-million ounces a year. Yet America's own production and reserves are minimal, and its stockpile is only enough for about one year's normal consumption, or 2 years' "critical needs."

Canada produces platinum as a by-product of nickel mining, but its output is a fraction of U.S. requirements, and could not easily be expanded. Only 2 countries have platinum on any scale—South Africa and the Soviet Union (though it has also been discovered in Rhodesia). Between them, they account for 93 per cent of the world production, with South Africa dominant in the supply of platinum itself and Russia leading in palladium.

Charles River Associates reported in 1976 that because of the level of stocks, use of recycled metal and usage economies, "the most important end-use industries would not be severely affected by even a total embargo on supplies of new platinum metals to the U.S. of up to 2 years." However, "a more enduring embargo could cause some severe problems." For instance, there are no immediately feasible non-platinum catalytic processes that could be used in the petroleum refining industry.

Manganese is essential in the manufacture of almost all steels to control sulfur and oxygen impurity levels and to improve quality, being used in a proportion averaging 13 lbs to the ton in the U.S., 20 lbs/ton in other Western countries. It is also the cheapest means of strengthening steel without loss of ductility, high-manganese steels being used for drill tips, cutting edges and railroad equipment. Manganese can only be substituted in most of its uses at great cost and loss of quality. Charles River Associates estimated that even a quadrupling or quintupling of the current price would only lead to economies that would cut consumption by one-fourth after a 4-year adjustment period. Manganese is also used in alloys with other metals such as aluminum and copper to impart qualities such as corrosion resistance, strength, electrical resistance, elasticity or anti-vibration characteristics. Small amounts are used in electrical batteries and the chemical industry.

The U.S. has no manganese. It is totally dependent on imports, either in the form of ore or already processed into ferro-manganese. It buys $1\frac{1}{2}$ million tons a year, worth about $190-million in 1975, and has a stockpile equivalent to about 2 years' normal consumption. South Africa is easily the largest producer in the non-Communist world, providing about one-third of supply. Russia is an even bigger producer, but most of its output is consumed within the Soviet bloc. There are other Free World suppliers. But, says Charles River Associates: "South Africa is crucial because its market share is more than twice that of Brazil, Gabon or Australia, and it has massive reserves sufficient in the long run to satisfy the current rate of Western consumption for more than a century." A 15 per cent cut in world manganese supply would initially force up the price $6\frac{1}{2}$ times and would cost the U.S. almost $1-billion over 15 years; a 26 per cent supply cutback would initially force up the price $10\frac{1}{2}$ times, and cost the U.S. almost $2-billion.

Other minerals in which South African supplies are important to the United States are vanadium, asbestos, antimony and vermiculite.

Vanadium is also used mainly to impart particular qualities

—especially exceptional toughness—to steels and other metals. A titanium alloy containing vanadium is used in missile and airplane components. Cast irons containing vanadium are used in the blocks, chilled iron rolls and diesel engine pistons. Consumers outside the metallurgical industries are chemicals and oil refining.

The U.S. mines vanadium, but not enough for its needs. In 1974 40 per cent of requirements were provided by imports, and more than half of these came from South Africa, which is easily the world's largest producer. Other suppliers are Namibia and Finland.

Asbestos is in heavy demand worldwide for use in building materials (pipes and sheets), brake linings and products needing fire-resistance. The U.S. mines asbestos on a small scale, but imported 87 per cent of its requirements in 1974. Canada is the world's major supplier. South Africa ranks second, and is the only supplier of the amosite and crocidolite varieties.

Antimony is a metal with unusual characteristics used in batteries and flame-proofing of automobile cables and upholstery. The U.S. is almost entirely dependent on imports. South Africa, Bolivia, Communist China and Russia are the largest producers.

Vermiculite is a flaky material which is becoming increasingly important for flame-proof and acoustic control products. The U.S. and South Africa are the only producers of significance, but the U.S. consumes the material on such a scale that it is South Africa's major customer.

In one important mineral—uranium—South Africa and the U.S. are shaping up as competitors. The U.S. is anxious to control sales of enriched uranium to prevent international proliferation of nuclear bomb capability, and probably also for commercial advantage—though it never admits to this.

Natural uranium contains only 0.7 per cent of the essential 235 isotope. Most nuclear power stations are fueled by enriched uranium, in which the 235 content has been raised to between 2 and 4 per cent. It doesn't sound much, but the enrichment process is technologically most complex and requires enormous and extremely expensive plants.

At present the U.S. supplies about 90 per cent of the enriched uranium going into nuclear power plants around the world. Almost all the rest comes from the Soviet Union, and Western countries are naturally unwilling to become dependent on that source. Consequently the U.S. still has a high degree of effective control over the world's nuclear power industry.

This will change during the Eighties as other industrially advanced countries build enrichment plants. But the U.S. is likely to be able to continue to exercise strong influence over them. Firstly, because they will still need a flow of enriched uranium from the U.S. in addition to the material they produce themselves. Secondly, because most of the raw uranium will come from countries that are likely to cooperate closely with the U.S.—Canada and Australia. There is the prospect, therefore, that the U.S. will continue to lead a "nuclear club" of uranium producing and enriching nations.

The odd man out in all this is South Africa, which is estimated to have the world's third largest reserves of uranium after the U.S. and Australia, and is forecast to become the second biggest producer in the early Eighties. If it manages to continue to exercise significant influence over the uranium marketing policies of an independent Namibia, its leverage will be that much greater (the only possible alternative *patron* would be the Soviet Union, which the U.S. would hardly welcome).

South African and Namibian production of uranium oxide totalled 2,800 tonnes in 1975. It is expected to reach 10,000 tonnes by the end of 1978. Resources are such that it should be possible to continue providing about one-sixth of the world's uranium supplies.

Not only will South Africa control substantial supplies of uranium oxide—it will also almost certainly build its own enrichment plant to come on stream in the later Eighties.

As South Africa has developed its own enrichment technology, and is therefore not beholden contractually to the U.S. or anyone else to observe the strict controls usually insisted on had it ratified the nuclear anti-proliferation treaty (which, like many other countries, it has refused to do), it will be free to market its enriched as well as its raw uranium in any way it wishes. This will put the country in a pivotal position. It will be in a position either to join the "nuclear club," or not to. If it does not, it would severely reduce the effectiveness of any U.S.-led coordinating body.

It is not surprising that leading South Africans see their minerals as trump cards in any bargaining with the United States.

15.

What America should do

The United States' policy toward South Africa is full of irony. At the time when White opinion was most inflexible and racism was still respectable within the country, Washington applied no real pressure. Now that Whites are ready to accept, and are already accepting, far-reaching changes in racial relationships, Washington is beginning to exert the kind of blatant pressure than could spark off a White backlash and bring the necessary process of liberalization to a halt.

The signs are already there. Before the Carter Administration began to threaten the South African Government, there was a mood favoring change in Pretoria, epitomized by Prime Minister Vorster's commitment "to investigate measures which are alleged to be irritating, injurious and discriminating and, if so found, to eliminate them." By July 1977 the mood had already changed to the degree that the Government ruled that no Black managers would be allowed at shops in White areas. Before the threats, few considered Dr. Andries P. Treurnicht, the able leader of the rigidly traditional wing of the ruling National Party, a serious contender for the premiership on John Vorster's retirement. By mid-1977, Deputy

Minister Treurnicht had emerged as a very real possibility as the man who might lead South Africa into laager.

Any policy of confrontation with South Africa would contain within it the seeds of tragedy, particularly for South Africa's Blacks. Any measures damaging the economy, for instance, would hurt Blacks far more than Whites, as it is they whose levels of employment and living standards are most sensitive to economic vigor. It is all very well for Administration officials to argue, as they have with South African envoys, that "we don't mind if we hit the Blacks now. Their sacrifices will be short term, because they'll bounce up when we've broken you." It is not they who will have to make the sacrifices. And the people who will, South Africa's Blacks, don't appear anxious to do so ... apart from a few young radicals who either don't realize how much suffering would be involved, or don't care.

Carter's envoy, Ambassador Young, has suggested that South African Blacks should boycott White business to bring about political change, because this technique worked in the U.S. South. If he was serious about this (he promptly went out and bought himself a South African-made suit, shirts and neckties), he shows astonishing ignorance of South African conditions. Blacks just do not have the resources to see through a confrontation with the White authorities, whether by means of boycotts or strikes. Not only would they suffer terribly, but they would precipitate White backlash. Even if the business community's will to resist were to crumble, the Government's would not—businessmen have far less political power in South Africa than they do in the U.S.

There is a high degree of interdependence of Black and White in the South African economy. If Blacks attempted to exploit their leverage for political purposes, they would be more likely to precipitate Black/White partition than White capitulation to majority rule. The result would be far greater suffering for Blacks than for Whites, as happened in Angola and Mozambique when Whites fled Black rule, and as could happen in Rhodesia if things go wrong there. Even the Russians now privately recognise this ugly consequence. If reports reaching South Africa from Europe are to be believed, they are now anxious that no more Whites should be driven out of Africa, or even out of the territories where they now live. Angola and Mozambique are big enough responsibilities. They don't want to have to pick up the pieces in Rhodesia, Namibia, even

South Africa, as well.

The essence of the Administration's rationalization of its policy toward South Africa is that if Blacks achieve "full participation" in the South African system, there is no danger of a Communist takeover. But the argument is riddled with flaws. Firstly, Whites fear Black majority rule as much or perhaps even more than Communism. Secondly, most of the Black leaders who have taken over in White Africa or threaten to are in any case Marxist, or close to being so. Nelson Mandela, for instance, has written: "The people of South Africa led by Communism will destroy the capitalist society." Thirdly, Soviet influence is increasing throughout Africa, including countries that do not have a Black/White problem, such as Ethiopia. Fourthly, there is no evidence that the majority of Blacks are prepared to go as far as revolution to throw Whites out of power, or even wish to throw them out of power at all.

The U.S. fears racial violence in Southern Africa, yet its refusal to support the few moderate Black leaders who are prepared to work with the White authorities to bring about evolutionary progress (such as the homeland leaders in South Africa, Rhodesia's Bishop Abel Muzorewa and ZUPO leader Jeremiah Chirau, the Turnhalle group in Namibia), and its pandering to the revolutionary leaders (such as the young Soweto radicals, the Patriotic Front, and Swapo), is like pouring gasoline on smoldering timber. It cuts the ground from under those prepared to compromise, boosts the morale of those who seek radical solutions, stiffens the resistance of Whites to change, and helps set the stage for a violent confrontation that would defeat and destroy the Black movements.

It was Gatsha Buthelezi, leader of Africa's most martial tribe and uncompromising critic of the South African Government, who said that to precipitate armed revolution among Blacks would "lead to certain suicide." He said that those foreigners advocating such a course showed "the height of irresponsibility"—especially as they themselves seemingly intend to stay safely well away from "the theater of this proposed violent confrontation." Those foreign observers who are knowledgeable about the security apparatus of the South African state, the latent power of its armed forces, and the determination of Whites not to become the subjects of a Black government that would almost inevitably be a dictatorship, know

133

that such a revolt could only fail. But its occurrence would also poison relations between Black and White in South Africa to such an extent as to set back for a century the whole process of intergroup adjustment. It would also alienate Black Africa from the U.S. and other Western nations.

A Black revolution that failed, leaving White South Africa surviving as an independent nation but isolated from the world, would have incalculable consequences for the West. It would leave Black America nursing a deep sense of racial grievance. It would do even more harm to America's prestige than the defeat in Vietnam, weakening America's global influence. It would alienate the Third World generally, and Black Africa particularly, from the West. Although South Africans are not a vindictive people, they would certainly not easily forgive and forget those nations which had been ranged against them, and the West's material interests in South Africa would be gravely prejudiced by a hostility that they themselves precipitated. The Republic would be hard, intractable, closed to external influences ... and perhaps dangerously self-confident. Western nations, having based their policies on the assumption that South Africa would collapse in a comparatively short time, would have to pick up most of the tab for their misjudgement. A heavy one.

Fortunately there are many liberals within the U.S. and in Europe who, while sharing much of the Carter Administration's thinking, foresee these dangers and suspect that Washington is suffering from the traditional American weakness for instant solutions ... that with the best combination of pressures on Pretoria, change will only come slowly. The British Foreign Secretary David Owen, for instance, who is certainly not sympathetic towards the South African Government, has said: "It took some decades before the White South and Southern opinion in America could come to grips with the need to treat Black Americans as their equals and to give them full civil rights. That struggle, for instance, was still going on in the 1960s. Now I think in South Africa it is going to take a long time to make those changes and we in the West are going to have to understand this and we're going to have to try and persuade Black Africa to understand this."

So, what should the U.S. do? Many Americans argue that the U.S. cannot openly back the existing White-controlled authorities because of moral repugnance, the hostility of Black Americans, the crippling burden that formalized racism represents in any contest with Communism, and South Africa's loser's image. But neither can it hope to compete with the Soviet Union in any contest of extremes to gain the support of the Black radical challengers who (notwithstanding occasional denials) are strongly Marxist, anti-American, and determined to impose political systems repugnant to decent Americans.

The United States' natural allies in Africa ought to be moderate Blacks, who should represent an acceptable alternative to both White minorities and Black radicals. Admittedly, there are great practical difficulties with this approach. There are not many politically sophisticated and politically-involved moderate Black Africans. They lack the guns, the money and the determination of the White minorities and the Black radicals. When they cooperate with the White authorities, as in the epoch-making Turnhalle constitutional negotiations in Namibia, they are castigated as sell-outs and Uncle Toms and are denied the diplomatic support they should expect from the U.S. When they cooperate with the Black radicals, they tend to become pawns in the hands of Moscow-trained manipulators, and to lose political integrity in the eyes of the Whites who hold the power.

In choosing who to back and how to back them in the stormy uncertainties of Southern Africa, U.S. foreign policymakers face a baffling tangle of complex and sometimes contradictory interests. It's not surprising that the policy often seems so muddled as to be incomprehensible.

The U.S. has always been limited in the extent to which it can exert negative leverage on South Africa. It has already thrown some of those levers, for instance by banning arms sales and prohibiting Eximbank credits. It now seems to be contemplating throwing its remaining negative levers, such as stopping capital flows and driving down the gold price. Such measures will be no more effective than the previous ones, because they under-estimate both the capacity and the determination of White South Africa to resist outside pressure. The U.S. will end up without any negative levers left to throw, and with less influence than ever over Pretoria, because by then Pretoria will regard Washington as an enemy capital.

Yet the U.S. has an enormous potential leverage on South Africa to bring about real change for the better. It does not even seem to be considering it, because the Administration is more interested in pandering to the emotions of South Africa's critics within the U.S. and around the world, than it is in actually advancing the interests of South African Blacks. That potential lies in the realm of positive leverage—the reverse of the policies that the U.S. has been pursuing.

The concept is a simple one: That in human affairs, and particularly when dealing with proud and stubborn foreign nations, the carrot is a more effective motivator than the stick. Here is how it might work between the U.S. and the Republic. Washington ought to be saying to Pretoria something like this: "Here is a list of the 8 most important changes that we would like to see in South Africa. If you implement any one of these to our satisfaction, then we shall reward you by making a significant positive change in our policy toward you, on the basis of our selection from a list submitted by you, if you go even part of the way toward meeting one of your requests."

The American list might look something like this:

● A blueprint, with a firm timetable, for the evolution of a system of full participation by Blacks, Coloreds and Asians in the government of South Africa.
● Acceptance of United Nations' authority over Namibia.
● Compliance with U.N. sanctions against Rhodesia.
● Accession to and compliance with the Nuclear Non-Proliferation Treaty.
● Repeal of the anti-miscegenation clause of the Immorality Act and of the Mixed Marriages Act.
● Abolition of all forms of job reservation.
● A firm timetable, with a short time-span, for abolition of ethnic discrimination in public service pay scales.
● A commitment to increase spending each year on Black education at twice the rate of increase in spending on White education.

The South African list might look something like this:

● Removal of the ban on sales of U.S. arms to the Republic.
● Federal Government guarantee of large commercial loans ($5-billion?) to provide funds for the social and economic development of Blacks, Coloreds and Asians.

- A firm financial and military commitment to support a coalition of Black and White moderates in Rhodesia, should power be transferred to them by means of an internal settlement.
- A similar commitment to the Turnhalle group in Namibia.
- Diplomatic recognition of the Transkei, and of other homelands as they become dependent nations.
- A defense treaty between the U.S. and South Africa.
- A commitment to make no further free market sales of U.S. Treasury gold, and to oppose further gold sales by the IMF.
- A program of positive encouragement of investment by U.S. corporations in South Africa, and removal of all discouragements such as the ban on Eximbank loans.

Now obviously compliance with any one of these items would be a major concession by either of the countries involved, so initially a positive leverage experiment might require much more modest "barter". For instance, South Africa might agree to abolish certain forms of job reservation in exchange for the freedom to purchase long-range naval reconnaissance airplanes. The two countries could proceed step by step, slowly building up confidence in each other's integrity, and adapting the program of objectives to conform to changing political, social and economic circumstances. It would be a policy of partnership instead of confrontation, of construction rather than destruction. Positive leverage, I believe, is the only way that the U.S. can have a significant impact on the South African domestic situation, and produce immediate and visible gains for South African Blacks, Coloreds and Asians.

Policies of excluding pariah nations from the world community have never worked favorably before, and in fact have often led to the most ghastly kinds of armed conflict. There is no reason to believe they will work favorably in South Africa's case. Let the last word on this topic rest with former Treasury Secretary William E. Simon (not a particular friend of South Africa's), who declared in June 1977: "It just doesn't make much sense, economically or diplomatically, to put South Africa into a deep-freeze, to exclude it from all forms of cooperation within the international community—casting it out, slamming the door, and pretending it doesn't exist.

"There is much about South Africa of which we may well be

137

critical. But it is only natural for people to listen to the criticism of those whom they see as their friends, not those whom they perceive as their adversaries. We should not seek to reduce cooperation with South Africa, but to extend it, thus utilizing South Africa's considerable human and physical resources in the interests of the international community while also exerting a positive influence on South African society.

"Does that mean that we accept South Africa's racial policies? Certainly not. I strongly disagree with many aspects of those policies. But I would suggest that human rights is not the central issue. If it were, I can hardly see how the Carter Administration could by cozying up to Cuba, where there are thousands upon thousands of political prisoners, while turning its back on South Africa. Indeed, Africa itself is a continent where political persecution, ethnic discrimination and undemocratic governments are widespread. It is a continent where the fires of democracy have long ago been dimmed.

"I can certainly see the advantage of the United States' pursuing an evenhanded policy in Southern Africa, trying to assist those people in working out a just and lasting settlement of their disputes—a settlement that will minimize hatred and bloodshed. But I see little advantage to us, to the West, or to any of the peoples of South Africa, in further isolating that country from the international community.

"The U.S. is currently involved in a wide-ranging reassessment of its relations with South Africa. In my view, that reassessment should lead to greater, not lesser, involvement with South Africa because that is the most effective and most humane way to bring about peaceful change."

16.

Why South Africa is singled out

Probably the greatest obstacle that South Africa faces in gaining American understanding of its position is that the whole American constitutional, political and social tradition has been the diametric opposite of South Africa's as a means of accommodating diverse cultural and ethnic groups within a single state.

With the exceptions of some miscegenation in the early years of European settlement that produced the Colored community, and of economic integration largely limited to master/servant and employer/worker relationships, South Africans have always tended to live apart. They have cleaved to their own cultural and ethnic communities, buttressing this natural separation with social sanctions and, over the past century, with laws. South African society is divided not only by race, but also by language, culture, value systems, religion, levels of education and socio-economic potential. No human society, it has been said, is as rich as South Africa's in its variety and diversity.

The most startling example of how deeply desired and defended is ethnicity in South Africa is not racial separation, but linguistic diversity. The most widely-used *home* language in South Africa is only spoken by 20 per cent of the country's population. It is Zulu.

Afrikaans, one of the official languages, is only spoken by about 19 per cent of people in South Africa as a home language; English, the second official language, by a mere 14 per cent; Xhosa by about 12 per cent; other tongues are the home languages of even smaller groups.

Americans tend to think of South Africa divided along Black/White lines, but there are deep divisions within the Black and Brown communities. The only vicious race riot in South African history was between Zulus (Blacks) and Asians. It took place in Durban in 1949. Hundreds died, and it was the White security forces who ended the rioting.

The entire course of South African history has been along the path of pluralism and diversity. The Nationalists did not create apartheid ("apartness") ... they structured separation, formalized it, turned it into an ideology, gave it an Afrikaans name that sounds ugly to English-speakers, and codified it (sometimes to the point of absurdity). Even if this process has now been reversed, there is no evidence that South Africa's races wish to abandon pluralism—only that they wish to reshape many aspects of its practical application. And even if South Africans as a whole chose to go all the way to total ethnic and cultural integration, well beyond the political and social integration that many now appear to desire, it would be many decades and perhaps several centuries before this could be achieved, because of the diversity of the population.

By contrast, Americans have a totally different approach. From the early days of settlement they believed in the melting-pot, and they largely succeeded in achieving it. They wiped out the majority of their Indians, then overwhelmed the survivors with a wave of settlers and immigrants deliberately destroying tribal culture and identity. They deculturalized their negro slaves, imposing the language, religion and values of the White majority, and they partially integrated them genetically, so that today the differences that remain between a Black and White American are marginal compared with the differences between a Black and a White South African.

The Americans insisted that European immigrants should largely reject their cultural traditions and adopt native American ones, and until recently ethnic origin (if different from that of the dominant Anglo-Saxon) was something to keep quiet about, and if possible disguise. By contrast with South Africa, which is now partitioning itself by giving independence to Black homelands, the Americans have always placed emphasis on the integrity of their expanding geographical base—they fought their bloodiest and nastiest war a century ago primarily to preserve their nation's political unity.

Measured against this background, it is hardly surprising that few Americans are convinced when South Africans argue in favor of plural approaches to the many problems of ethnic diversity. If Europe is quoted as an example of how even a single race can be divided by cultural differences into a multiplicity of separate nations, Americans are likely to respond that that is precisely why Europe has been cursed with repeated wars over the centuries.

The diversity of the South African population and the concept of a politically and socially compartmentalized society are difficult for Americans to comprehend, measured against the background of their own integrated society. Not that pluralism represents any kind of threat to American society—it has never been considered a serious option. Although there is new interest and pride in ethnic origins, especially among Blacks *(Roots)* but also among Whites, and there is still a high degree of social segregation as there has always been, there are no more than a handful of Americans who want to take ethnic exclusivity further than this. Americans are proud of their melting-pot society, and there is no reason why they should change it.

It is only logical that Americans should see majority rule as the right and proper political approach to the governance of an integrated democratic society. It has been their own assurance of freedom from the persecution from which their ancestors fled, and it has been the mechanism by which the White Anglo-Saxons, who happened to be in a numerical preponderance, were able to impose their language, culture and policies on ethnic minorities. It is also logical that the White settlers in Southern Africa, who have always been in a minority, should prefer a very different political, social and cultural approach.

Unfortunately in the past and still today, separation has been so much a part of discrimination in South Africa that it is difficult to differentiate between the two. Indeed, there are many liberals who believe, as Vice-President Mondale said at Vienna, that separateness is inherently discriminatory. In fact, ethnicity is a worldwide phenomenon that South Africa did not create, and ethnicity is being expressed increasingly in political demands for self-rule or even independence through partitioning of territory (Quebec in Canada, Scotland and Wales in Britain, the Basques in Spain, the Palestinians in Israel). Nevertheless ethnicity in the South African context is seen somewhat simplistically by outsiders merely as an excuse for racism.

Among the many sins that human beings perpetrate against one another, discrimination on grounds of race has come to be viewed worldwide in recent years as the worst of all. This mystifies South Africans, as racism has caused very little violence and conflict around the world compared with politics (Vietnam, Indonesia, Nigeria, Israel, for example) and religion (India, Lebanon, Northern Ireland are instances). Hardly any of the millions of violent deaths in Africa in recent years have resulted from racial clashes.

Nevertheless, racism is widely regarded as the worst sin. More specifically, formalized discrimination by Whites against other races has become the worst sin, for formalized discrimination favoring Melanesians over Asians (Fiji), Malays over Chinese (Malaysia) and Blacks over Whites (Liberia), is not considered horrifying, nor a subject for condemnation at the United Nations.

Double standards of this kind infuriate South African Whites, who are still somewhat naive about the merciless realities of international politics and still have a greater belief than most in the principles they learned from their British imperial tutors (who, of course, were better at preaching them than practising them). South Africans still have to learn and to accept that double standards are inevitable in this imperfect world, as they reflect the reality of international political conditions—and that South Africa has to live with them, and adapt its policies to deal with them.

Obsession with White racism is, of course, a current fashion. But it is an obsession that is likely to remain in fashion for decades to come. It owes its importance as a political factor to many causes. Among the most important are the following.

Firstly, because of the increasing influence of universities in Western societies and of idealistic young people in setting social standards—an idealism that has only been able to flourish because of decades of unprecedented mass prosperity—there is an increasing concern in Western countries with human rights and democratic values. This has produced a strong distaste among ordinary decent human beings for discrimination against anyone on unreasonable grounds. Racism is seen by many as the worst form of discrimination because a man can change, hide or adapt his politics, religion or even social class to "get on"—but his skin color is an immutable badge.

Secondly, there is an acute sensitivity about all racial matters as a result of the horrible phenomenon of Nazi Germany, with its mass exterminations of "inferior" races. Many intelligent and sensitive Westerners even have a sense of shared guilt that this evil thing sprang from a deeply civilized European people and was initially tolerated by other Western nations.

Because of this "guilt by association", the humiliations inflicted on Blacks by Whites in Africa are judged far more harshly than widespread persecution and even extensive killing of Blacks by Blacks on the African continent. There is a degree of inverted racism in that Whites are *expected* to behave according to higher standards than Blacks. This is hardly surprising in the case of South Africa, whose constant references to "Western values" and to commendable aspects of its society such as stable administration, an independent judiciary and a free Press, infer that it expects to be judged by the standards of North America and Western Europe—not those of Africa or the Communist world.

Thirdly, there is a widespread feeling of guilt in Western countries—all of them largely or almost entirely inhabited by Whites—about their past or even present treatment of other races, either at home (Black Americans, Australian aborigines), or abroad (British, French and Dutch colonialism). This is especially prevalent in the Anglo-Saxon and Northern European countries, where centuries of Protestant influence have made feelings of guilt about many things (sexuality and idleness are examples) a driving force in national characters.

People in these countries are embarrassed that White Africans—whom they feel, to a greater or lesser degree, to be their kith and kin—are seemingly perpetuating the evil behavior of their past and reluctant present. For undoubtedly, despite decades of well-intentioned effort, racial problems are still far from solved in North America and Western Europe, and there is still widespread de facto discrimination against racial minorities. There is some element of subconscious desire to evade self-blame for this, by transferring blame to others.

Fourthly, there is the Third World. It sees South Africa as a relic of the colonial era, because Whites continue to rule other races there just as Whites used to rule others in their countries' colonies. South Africa is a symbol of a global White domination that has lasted for half a millenium as a result of superior organization and technology ... and still continues. It is therefore a focus for the Third World's resentment against that domination and what it has cost them culturally, politically, spiritually and economically. If South Africa didn't exist, if the Black majority took power, then Third World countries would find some other target for their resentment (the U.S. would be a prime candidate)—because they are powerless at present to end the superiority of the developed Western nations that is the basic cause of their frustration and feelings of inadequacy.

Against this background of strain, caused not only by racial tension but also the stark contrast between the great wealth and sybaritic wastefulness of the developed countries, and the grinding poverty of the Third World, it suits Western governments to divert the attentions of the Third World away from themselves and against a convenient scapegoat—South Africa.

The peculiar ethnic structure of its society made it inevitable that South Africa should be such a scapegoat, but to some extent it has also set itself up for this role by its ideological rigidities. W.B. Ofuateg-Kodjoe, a Black who is Professor of Political Science at the City University of New York, has commented caustically: "The preferred U.S. model for multiracial societies has been the more respectable one of maintaining White supremacy in an integration-ist/assimilationist context as is the case of the United States itself—if the Whites in the (South African) redoubt were to retreat from their position (of explicit White superiority), and to adopt the more internationally accepted integrationist/assimilationist model of White superiority advocated by the United States, they could avoid all the international censure."

Notwithstanding its many deficiencies, South Africa is an example of advanced material development, stable administration and human rights. But this is actually a cause of its poor relations with Black Africa. It is an embarrassing standard for comparison with the rest of the continent that other nations' rulers do not appreciate. What's more, they see White South Africa as an alien intrusion into Mother Africa that ultimately threatens them with its military and industrial might. They fear it in the same way as the Arabs fear the presence of the advanced state of Israel in the Middle East.

Some Black African leaders genuinely accept that South African

Whites are not colonialists, but truly Africans, who must work out their destiny on the continent because they have nowhere else to go. Many more are willing to accept this publicly (as in the Lusaka Declaration) for tactical reasons, because it neutralizes sympathy of the powerful Western peoples for African Whites, while privately thinking otherwise. But there is an element of subconscious or even conscious desire in many Black African leaders for revenge against South African Whites for their own real or imagined sufferings under White colonial rule, from which they were so recently released.

Fifthly, there is almost universal hostility among the politically-conscious toward the South African concept of an eventual plural democracy, with authority decentralized on an ethnic group basis, and political and social rights defined on a community rather than an individual basis. Homogeneous countries like Sweden and The Netherlands can't even begin to understand what such ideological complexities are about and view them simply as disguised racism.

There is a certain irony in the way racial minorities in other countries react with horror against apartheid. This is because they tend to identify with the Blacks, who are the apparent underdogs even though in a numerical majority. As Dr. Chris Barnard, the eminent heart surgeon, has pointed out, Black Americans should not identify themselves in South Africa with Blacks, because of race, but with the Whites, because they are also a minority. If Black Americans inherited a situation in which they controlled the U.S., even though in a minority, would they willingly hand over power to the White majority?

The concept of pluralism represents a real threat to the stability of many Third World countries with potentially serious ethnic minority problems, such as most of those in Africa. This is one reason why they are so hostile to the very concept of separate development, to the point where they refuse to recognize Transkei, a sovereign Black African state, every bit as viable economically and otherwise as dozens of other independent countries, because it is the firstborn of separate development's partition policy.

Many Third World countries came to independence with boundaries arbitrarily drawn by their former imperial rulers, often without cognisance of the pattern of settlement or wishes of the local population. Tribes divided by frontiers are commonplace throughout Africa. The linguistic and cultural differences are as strong

145

among the tribes of Africa as they are among the peoples of Europe. Therefore the post-colonial rulers feel an imperative need to prevent the flowering of ethnic identity and to promote the concept of single nationality among peoples of several different tribal "nations" if their countries are not to fragment and fly apart. Africa has already seen a cruel war fought, at the cost of the lives of 2-million people, in this very cause—Nigeria's successful campaign to prevent Biafra's breakaway.

A policy that recognizes, even praises, ethnic diversity, is bad news for Black Africa's leaders. A policy that takes it further, and even encourages tribes to break away and create their own independent countries, is even worse news. This is an important reason why Black Africa is so insistent that South Africa must pass to majority rule as a single integrated state, and not partitioned.

It is important to differentiate between genuine distaste, even disgust, over South African racial policies, and the cynical exploitation of these feelings for political and national advantage. For instance, many anti-South African militants are Marxists who see the destruction of the Republic as part of the subversion of the free enterprise system. Sometimes they give the game away, as in the 1972 book *The South African Connection,* which said: "It is not racialism as such that is the oppressor but the system of South African capitalism."

It can be argued, and often is, that South Africa has "asked for it," now that it faces a concerted campaign of international isolation led by the U.S., because of the way it has blatantly formalized racial discrimination, thus dredging up unfortunate memories of Nazi Germany, pushing discrimination to absurd extremes (such as segregated doorways leading on to common concourses, and preventing couples from marrying because one partner has crinkly hair). Undoubtedly such things have caused a great deal of hurt to human beings and unnecessary harm to the country's image. Undoubtedly South Africa has done some things that have been brutal, and a great many things that have been stupid. So have many other countries.

However, and notwithstanding what many critics of the South African Government argue, it is not apartheid that has made the country an object of international opprobrium. After all, Rhodesia is equally hated and more extreme measures have been mounted against it by the international community, yet Rhodesia has never

146

known anything like the degree of formal separation of the races that exists in South Africa, and the basic concept of its political system is integrationist, not pluralistic. The Portuguese, too, when they ruled in Africa, were attacked as harshly although they practised racial integration. The mounting offensive against South Africa is not to do with morality, but with currently fashionable views of national interest held in Washington and other world capitals. South Africa's response must be based on the same assumptions.

17.

Counter-attack

South Africa is a young nation compared with the United States, even though its roots go back almost as far (the Plymouth Pilgrims sailed only 32 years before the first Dutch settlers reached the Cape of Good Hope). South Africa only became united and self-governing in 1910, shortly after the bitterly-fought Boer War that pitched two small Afrikaner republics against the entire British Empire, and was in many ways like the Revolutionary War and the American Civil War rolled into one. The country only broke its remaining constitutional links with Britain when it became a republic in 1961.

As a result, colonial influences are still strong in its thinking. For instance, its newspapers are excessively full of reportage from Britain and scanty in their coverage of the U.S. and major non-English-speaking countries such as West Germany and Japan. The pattern of its social life is still so close to that of the British that South Africans travelling abroad (Afrikaners as well as Englikaners) feel more at home in Britain than anywhere else. Its economic policymakers are still heavily influenced by the laissez-faire ideas of Victorian England that are singularly unsuited to a semi-developed African country in a state of undeclared war. And its Foreign Service is often referred to scathingly by foreigners as a "pinstriped brigade" imitative of the British as they used to be.

All this is changing, of course. But very slowly. South Africa still behaves rather like a gawky and truculent teenager in its foreign policy, determined to show its independence, yet secretly yearning for the comfortable past when foreign relations were left to the British "parent".

South Africa has always seen itself as a loyal junior member of the Atlantic family of nations, and has behaved accordingly. Notwithstanding bitter internal dispute (it had its own version of America Firsters), South Africa was one of the first countries to follow Britain into war against Germany in 1939. It was a founder-member of the United Nations and its Prime Minister, Jan Smuts, helped draft the preamble to the Charter. It participated in the Berlin Airlift and it sent air squadrons to fight alongside U.S. forces in Korea. No doubt it would have fought in Vietnam, too, had it been asked. It wasn't.

South Africa has always supported the main Western countries in international forums, except on political issues involving Southern Africa. It is a responsible and law-abiding member of Western-orientated international institutions such as GATT and the IMF. Its system of government, judiciary, laws and way of life are patterned on those of the English-speaking democracies. "There is more Press freedom in South Africa than in the rest of Africa put together," says Frank Barton, Africa Director of the International Press Institute. South Africa was implacably opposed to Communism, whether of the Soviet or Chinese variety, long before Communism became a direct threat to its existence.

Despite all this, South Africa has been gradually excluded from the Western community of nations as hostility to its racial policies has mounted. Western countries have increasingly come to view the racism of African Whites as morally repugnant—and also dangerous to their own international interests.

In recent years South African policymakers have become more conscious of the obvious dangers of the country's increasing isolation. This has started to produce a more active and independent foreign policy, with a defensive campaign to maintain established links with traditional "friends", and attempts to build links with new "friends" in Africa and elsewhere.

Firstly, there have been "detente" initiatives to establish communication and where possible policy coordination with the leaders of Black African states. Secondly, there has been an active effort to

149

cultivate relations with individual minor or middle-ranking states not implacably opposed to South Africa, such as Israel, Iran, Taiwan and Paraguay. Thirdly, there have been more aggressive and sophisticated efforts at public relations in major countries that have traditionally been friendly, like the U.S., Britain, France and West Germany.

In Black Africa, the Republic has had rather more success than many observers expected, for a variety of reasons. One is that the posture of extreme hostility toward South Africa adopted by Black Africa in all its public statements does not reflect the rather more moderate feelings of many Black African leaders: extremist postures with moderate actions are part of the traditional cultural pattern across Africa, and the still-primitive political attitudes of their populations virtually obliges Black rulers to adopt anti-White stances. Another reason is that the Republic is a rich and militarily strong country, so African nations see immediate material advantages in friendly relations. A third is that a number of Black African leaders are strongly anti-Communist, do not share the U.S. Administration's unruffled unconcern about the Soviet move into Africa, and see the Republic's strong hostility to Communism as offsetting its racist vices. A fourth is a strong conviction held by many Black African leaders that South African Whites cannot be crushed by terrorism and broken by external pressures, and that the best way to cure them of their racist vices is through increased contact, friendship and cooperation.

At the height of the South African detente initiative in late 1974 and early 1975, Prime Minister Vorster flew twice to West Africa, for meetings with President William R. Tolbert of Liberia, President Félix Houphouët-Boigny of the Ivory Coast and President Léopold Senghor of Senegal. Senior South African officials privately met the leaders of other Black countries, including President Kenneth Kaunda of Zambia (in an initiative backed by Tanzania, Mozambique, Botswana and Malawi) and President Joseph-Desiré Mobutu Sese Seko of Zaire. During 1974 alone, it was subsequently revealed, South Africa had direct contact with more than a dozen Black African states and there were hundreds of exchange visits with these, ranging from ministerial level down to mid-range officials, scientists, and so on.

This activity has largely gone underground following the Angolan disaster, the escalation of Soviet influence in Africa, and the new international trend toward isolating the Republic. But, says Information Secretary Dr. Eschel Rhoodie: "These contacts still exist, have in fact increased, and dialogue with Black Africa is far from dead." Information Minister Mulder said in May 1977 that, through various Government departments, South Africa was liaising with "at least" 18 African and Middle East countries. President Houphouët-Boigny, South Africa's staunchest friend in West Africa, and ruler of one of the continent's few free-enterprise and prosperous states, still talks openly—Prime Minister Vorster briefed him on his talks with Vice-President Mondale immediately after leaving Vienna.

South Africa's trade with Black African countries, including many that supposedly ban such trade, is extensive. An average of 5 huge cargo planes leave Johannesburg's Jan Smuts Airport every day carrying cargo north to Black Africa. Israel, in an attempt to expose the hypocrisy of its Black African critics, told the U.N. in October 1976 that 19 African countries, including Nigeria, Angola, Mozambique, Liberia and Ghana, were doing close to $800-million worth of business a year with South Africa. It claimed that the Republic was even secretly propping up the Zambian economy by paying Iran direct for oil supplied to Zambia.

What is no secret is that South Africa keeps Mozambique's economy ticking over by providing 80 per cent of its foreign exchange and technicians to keep harbors and railroads operating; exports oil, foodstuffs, chemicals and spares to Zaire by rail and air, while providing transport facilities for export of Zairese copper; and is active with trade, aid and services in Zambia, Malawi, Gabon, Central African Empire ... even Angola. Some large South African companies claim that substantial proportions of their turnover come from sales to Black Africa. The neighboring Black states of Botswana, Lesotho, Swaziland and Transkei are so economically dependent on South Africa that they are united with it in customs and monetary unions.

Outside Africa, the Republic has tried to win friends among the smaller anti-Communist powers. The most important and successful of these initiatives has undoubtedly been toward Israel, where years of building unpublicized and sometimes secret relations in a number of fields culminated in a state visit to Israel April 1976 by Prime Minister Vorster. One result was the establishment of machinery for regular consultation between the two countries in the economic, industrial and scientific fields.

Neither side wants to talk about it, but there is much speculation about military cooperation, too. According to Western diplomats, Israel "has sold some of its most sophisticated weapons, including gunboats and guided missiles, to South Africa." South African newspapers have reported that the Republic is believed to have placed about $115-million worth of orders with Israel's arms industries. The *Financial Gazette* reported: "South Africa has looked into the possibility of buying Israel's Kfir fighter-bomber, but dropped the idea when the United States indicated it would block exports of the jet's American-made engine. South Africa has helped pay for the weapons by providing uranium for atomic bombs believed to have been produced at Israel's secret Dimona nuclear center. Marcia Freedman, an outspoken member of Israel's Parliament, says the Jewish state has also sent hundreds of military advisers to help train South Africa's armed forces, presumably in counter-insurgency techniques."

South Africa's relationship with Israel has long been a warm one. It was one of the first countries to recognize the Jewish state, and it has supplied men, money and materials to Israel at every time of crisis from the War of Independence to the Yom Kippur conflict. There is a strongly pro-Zionist Jewish community of some 120,000 which raises a lot of money for Israel and is allowed to transfer the funds easily, despite exchange control, by a sympathetic Government. South African gentiles are about the most pro-Israel you will find anywhere, perhaps because the obvious parallels between the situations of the two countries produce a strong sense of identification. In 5 years trade between South Africa and Israel has risen fivefold, to more than $100-million in 1976, with Israel buying materials such as coal and iron and selling manufactures such as electrical equipment, textiles and chemicals.

Rather more discreet is South Africa's growing relationship with Iran. There is a sentimental connection in that the father of the Shah of Iran was exiled to South Africa during the Second World War by the British, and was so well treated that the Pahlevi family has been well-disposed toward the country ever since. The Republic buys most of its oil from Iran, but the relationship has gone beyond straight trade. Iran has a 15 per cent stake in a large oil refinery controlled by the South African Government, and Iranian students now study at the Afrikaans University of Pretoria. Iran is recruiting

152

South African artisans and technicians to develop a large copper mine, and buying a wide range of South African products from cement to trailers.

Relations are also improving with Taiwan, the Far Eastern country most friendly toward South Africa. Both countries are staunchly anti-Communist and face increasing international isolation. Two-way trade has doubled almost every year since 1972, and the Republic of China is now second to Japan in size as a Far East market for South African goods. Taiwan is the only Far East country to exchange ambassadors with the Republic, and collaboration between the two has extended beyond commercial matters.

South Africa has devoted considerable effort in recent years to improving its relations with Latin America, with fair success among the smaller nations. Prime Minister Vorster has paid official visits to Uruguay and Paraguay, and President Alfredo Stroessner of Paraguay has visited the Republic. Pretoria has diplomatic or consular relations with Panama, Guatemala, Costa Rica, Nicaragua and El Salvador. Business links have been growing faster, and on a broader basis, with a certain amount of official aid to assist. A South African construction firm has a $54-million share in Peru's Majes irrigation and hydropower project, two fertilizer companies are opening up a substantial market for their phosphoric acid in Brazil, and another concern is building a cement works in Uruguay. These are just a few examples.

Of course the U.S. remains the No. 1 target for South Africa's endeavors to improve its foreign relations. Not only because of its immense political, military and economic power, but also because the other major Western nations and Japan tend to follow its lead in dealing with the Republic. Not surprisingly the country's ablest diplomat, "Pik" Botha, was sent to Washington as ambassador for several years, and when he was recalled in 1977 it was to become Foreign Minister. He was succeeded by a top career diplomat, Donald B. Sole, while Botha himself remains a frequent visitor to the States.

Because of the change in Washington's South Africa policies in recent years, and the growing interest in the South African issue by radical groups now the U.S. has disengaged from Vietnam, and other Southern African issues like the Portuguese colonies, Rhodesia and Namibia are regarded as resolved or well on the way to being resolved, the Republic is fighting an essentially defensive battle in the U.S.

Its principal political objective is no more than to keep open lines of communication to the Administration, the Congress, and to other parties who influence the shaping of U.S. foreign policy; to promote understanding of the extreme complexity of Southern African problems and to counter radical propaganda. A good example of the kind of activity being undertaken was the economic seminar held in New York in June 1977 by the South African Foreign Trade Organization and the Republic's largest investment bank, Senbank, which was attended by almost 300 representatives of U.S. corporations with investments in South Africa. They listened to addresses by South African leaders such as Reserve Bank Senior Deputy Governor Dr. Gerhard de Kock, Ciskei Chief Minister Lennox Sebe and labor union chief Arthur Grobbelaar, and mixed informally with White, Black and Brown businessmen from the Republic.

There can be no doubt that more of this kind of information-spreading activity is essential in the U.S., where there is considerable ignorance of Southern African realities, even among those where one would not expect to find it. For instance, the South African newspaperman Ton Vosloo, when he visited the U.S. in May 1977, was asked by a policymaker in the Administration questions that betrayed amazing ignorance. For instance: "It is true that you Whites speak two languages?" "Is Botswana an independent country?" And: "Does Mr. Oppenheimer support the opposition?"

(Harry Oppenheimer, chairman of the huge Anglo American Corporation, has been an active public supporter of the anti-apartheid Progressive Federal Party and its predecessors since he was a young man.)

One of South Africa's specific objectives in its diplomatic offensive is to convince the U.S. that it should continue to use its veto in the U.N. Security Council to block any resolutions that, if passed, would oblige all U.N. members to impose sanctions against South Africa. At present sanctions have been voted for by the General Assembly, but such resolutions merely recommend, and member-nations are not obliged to comply with them in terms of the Charter. South Africa is also anxious that the U.S. should not express official support for Black revolutionary movements in Africa, which South African Whites see as Communist, totalitarian, anti-White racist, and committed to violence.

In the economic sphere, the Republic is anxious to prevent additional sanctions of any kind being imposed by the U.S. (several mild ones have been applied, such as a ban on Eximbank credits); to encourage American concerns to expand their investments in South Africa; and to develop trade and physical communications between the two countries.

South Africa's strategic interests in the U.S. are mainly concerned with arms supplies. The U.S. imposed a ban on sales of weapons in 1963 (lobbyist DeKieffer refers to this caustically as the French Arms Dealers' Relief Act, as it merely diverted South African purchasing from American suppliers to French ones). South Africa would not like to see this extended to civilian goods with military applications, such as aircraft, trucks and computers. Indeed, it would like to see it relaxed, for instance to allow South Africa to buy Orion long-distance naval reconnaissance planes, which could not possibly be used against the internal population or guerilla invaders, and would actually provide a payoff to the U.S. in improving intelligence on Soviet shipping movements in the South Atlantic and Indian oceans. The Republic also hopes to convince Washington that it should not exert pressure on allies such as France and Israel to stop selling weapons to it. And it would like the U.S. to see the wisdom of making use of South African naval and air force bases, especially now it has lost its last base in the Arab world (Bahrein) and has few friendly territories it can use south of the Middle East oilfields.

What degree of success South Africa will have with its diplomatic offensive, only time will tell. But there are signs of an alternative gameplan shaping up in the minds of South African policymakers. That they are no longer mentally locked into the "friendly dog" posture of the past ("Please don't kick me—I really do love you").

18.

Options for South Africa

Dramatic evidence of South African disenchantment with the U.S. and its foreign policy was the publication in the largest-circulating Afrikaans newspaper, Rapport, in May 1977, of an article by John H. Chettle. Chettle is no Government spokesman. But neither is he a lightweight. He is the Washington-based Director for North and South America of the South Africa Foundation, a private organization with powerful backing from the business community that seeks to promote international understanding of the Republic without having to defend official race policies. Chettle is typical of the Foundation's officers based overseas—highly intelligent, perceptive, balanced and persuasive. The views he expressed were his own, not the Foundation's. But they reflect in some ways, and are ahead of in others, the views of a number of people in and close to the centers of power in Pretoria.

"It is hard to think of any time since the settlement at the Cape when the dangers confronting us have been greater," he wrote. "We have to reconstruct our society to provide a focus for the aspirations of all our peoples at a time of deep division, international isolation and economic depression. These circumstances have given rise to a belief which is perhaps the most dangerous of all: the belief that the present system in South Africa will inevitably collapse in violence.

"At this critical moment an American Administration has been elected which is committed to human rights, heavily indebted to the Black vote, and determined to take action on South Africa. There can be few people who have any knowledge of the workings of the American Government who do not realize the danger for South Africa.

"Many South Africans see the solution to this crisis in internal change in South Africa, and in the elimination of petty apartheid. Others emphasize the need to find a permanent and accepted constitutional structure. Others believe that we have to discourage action against us by making ourselves militarily powerful. These are all aspects of the truth, but they are not enough. We need to do all these things. But we need to change our foreign policy as well.

"Our anti-Communism, far from helping us, is regarded by many of those who hold the power in the U.S. as being unfashionable ... an outmoded and even embarrassing reminder of the excesses of their McCarthy era." South Africans said to the U.S., in effect, that although it condemned them, refused to sell arms to them, would not let its navy use their ports, denied them trade loans and attacked the role of gold in the international monetary system ... they would always remain faithful. The U.S. could still use Simonstown (the naval base near Cape Town) when it wished, it could continue to have free access to South African minerals, and South Africa would never gang up against the U.S. in mineral cartels.

"It is one of the most uncelebrated love stories in history—and one of the most futile," Chettle wrote. "We are like the ardent swain who assures his beloved that, however she may spurn him, however unfaithful she may be, he will remain true. That may be very admirable, but it is not necessarily the best way to win a woman, nor to win an ally."

South Africa had to look to its own national interests—not the interests of other countries, or ideological principles. The country should, for the first time, apply to its foreign policy the rallying-cry of onetime premier and political hero General James B. Hertzog, who once led the movement to free the country from its colonial subjection to Britain: "South Africa First."

As a major raw materials producer, South Africa should take the lead in demanding higher prices from the developed countries, instead of supporting those countries against the Third World.

157

South Africa should "champion the interests of the poor and the downtrodden." This would produce political as well as economic benefits. "We possess, in our mineral resources, the most effective single weapon by which we can challenge the attitudes prevailing abroad," Chettle said. "The influence of Saudi Arabia, for example, is a direct reflection of the importance of her mineral and financial resources, though she is small and undeveloped otherwise. That importance has arisen, quite simply, from the operation of a cartel.

"A change in our attitude to the Soviet Union is implicit in such a strategy. If we want to take advantage of our mineral resources we have to deal with Russia. Russia has, for example, the largest reserves in the world, after ourselves, of manganese and chromite." Russia, he said, had shown itself to be a very practical country. "Indeed, in many respects the Soviet Union is a far less ideological country than the United States." The most obvious example of this was the Molotov-Ribbentrop Pact of 1939 between the Soviet Union and Nazi Germany.

But the Soviet Union was only a very practical country "when it is dealing with power, and when it has concrete objectives in view." Therefore South Africa might be able to deal with the Russians "only if we have shown that we are even more formidable militarily—and for that and other reasons it is almost imperative to have nuclear weapons."

Chettle concluded: "This is essentially a Gaullist foreign policy. The foundations for such a policy are perhaps even stronger in South Africa than they were in France. There is a deep sense of anger and betrayal in South Africa about the attitude taken towards us by our former allies." An active national-interest foreign policy "would give us a new flexibility in world affairs, it would divert attention from our racial problems, it would build up our financial and industrial power, it would create new links with the Third World, it would enable us to balance between East and West, and it would show that we cannot be taken for granted."

The Chettle commentary is not an isolated example of the development of a disenchantment and cooler South African attitude toward the U.S. and other Western countries. Prime Minister Vorster has said that if the U.S. is going to disown South Africa, then "I have no option but to go it alone. It's not by my choice, but I'm not going to shirk it. I don't mind being kicked in the pants—I'm quite used to that—but I'm damned if I'm going to be kicked in the teeth all the time."

Defense Minister Pieter W. Botha has warned that "it must not be taken for granted that South Africa will take part in a war on the side of the West. If it suits us, we can remain neutral. In the future we will have to act more independently as a country." Information Minister Mulder has said in Parliament that if South Africa continues to have blows rained on it by so-called "friendly" Western countries, then it will have to start thinking of "sailing under another flag." He went on: "It's time for America to wake up—or does there have to be another Pearl Harbor?"

John Barratt, Director of the South African Institute of International Affairs, has called for a declaration of neutrality. "There no longer seems to be any need for South Africa to commit itself in advance, as it were, to any particular powers, or to align itself with any particular group, except when special circumstances and its own interests so dictate." Dr. Jan du Plessis of the Foreign Affairs Association has pointed out the irony that the U.S. officially discriminates against loans to South Africa, yet Western loans to Communist countries reached about $27-billion in 1976, according to a NATO estimate. "Surely, if this kind of money could flow to your enemies, your friends are entitled to a few crumbs?"

In October 1976 the chief foreign correspondent of *Newsweek* magazine, Arnaud de Borchgrave, reported that the influential Bureau for State Security "believes that Vorster must make overtures to the Soviet Union in order to protect his flanks." This was dismissed as "nonsense" by the Bureau, which said it had never talked to De Borchgrave. Nevertheless it is a fact that there have been contacts between the South African and Russian governments, and there is already limited cooperation between the two countries in the marketing of diamonds and platinum. Rumors circulating in Southern Africa and in the U.S. have it that the Russian asking price for a deal with South Africa is abolition of legalized racial discrimination (never mind if discrimination continues informally); Blacks in nominal positions of authority in the national government (Whites can continue to exercise the real power); and some indication of acceptance of socialist principles, such as nationalization of the gold mining industry (which in practise would not be greatly different from the existing system of Government controls and "milking" of profits via taxes).

Such a package is hardly likely to appeal to South Africa. This in fact is one of the principal weaknesses in the case being argued for the "Soviet option." Undoubtedly Moscow would be delighted to have Africa's most powerful country as its ally, rather than a gaggle of comic-opera states with their arms locked in the Third World Salute (arms extended in supplication, with open palms). But clasping South Africa to its bosom would require an ideological about-turn every bit as wrenching as at the time of the Molotov-Ribbentrop Pact. The price demanded of the Republic for this would be more than South Africans would be willing to pay.

Besides, the Soviet Union may consider a permanent posture of total hostility toward South Africa, without any serious attempt to overthrow White rule, more advantageous to its national interests than either a deal with Pretoria, or majority-rule-type chaos as in Mozambique and Angola. This situation would help Russia to maintain and expand its influence in the Third World in exactly the same way that Israel's existence helps it in the Arab world. From Russia's point of view, both are like festering sores—so long as they continue to fester, the patient keeps going back to the doctor for treatment and consolation (arms and ideology). Without the sores, there would be no need of the doctor. Therefore this particular doctor has an interest in ensuring that his treatment doesn't go so far as actually removing the sores.

Notwithstanding the Administration's protestations that the U.S. will never go to South Africa's defense, Moscow views the Republic as a significant outpost of the West and does not believe that the "New York capitalists" would fail to come to the aid of South Africa if it really came to the crunch. This is another reason why we can expect the Soviet Union to desist from seeking to break South Africa by brute military force.

Information Minister Mulder has hinted at, and others have openly suggested, a working relationship with Communist China rather than Communist Russia. But while Moscow could at least provide Pretoria with major payoffs if it were willing to do a deal (removal of the only potentially serious military threat to the Republic, dislocation of the subversive Black revolutionary movements, and the economic advantages of minerals cartels), Peking could offer nothing more than friendly influence with Third World governments, even if it were interested. Military, economically and even politically, Communist China is a paper tiger—the epithet, ironically, that it invented to apply to others.

Both the Soviet and Chinese options are also unrealistic because they could not be "sold" to South African Whites, who exercise their influence through the highly democratic structure of their community's political system. South African Whites are politically conservative, they favor free enterprise, they are still deeply Christian people, and they have been brought up on an unremitting diet of strident anti-Communism for one-third of a century. They are not cynical and opportunistic enough to support their leaders in any "deal with the devil" except under the most extreme circumstances, which are unlikely to occur.

The most intriguing foreign policy alternative for South Africa was spelled out by American columnist Jeffrey Hart in June 1976. He suggested that international pressure on the "pariah states"—Israel, South Africa, Iran, Taiwan and possibly in time also Brazil and Turkey—could give rise to a new geographical grouping that he called the Fifth World. This could result from their international isolation and their declining faith in U.S. support in a crisis. Such a grouping of nations, Hart pointed out, could pool powerful military and economic forces. These states "do not often end up on the winning side of 'world opinion,' but they command advanced technology, a big slice of the world's natural resources, and strategic position astride vital sea routes, plus that rare quality in the present Western world: political will."

There is surely something in this concept. Those countries with the most difficult arms supplies problems and whose existence is most threatened by these problems—Israel, South Africa, South Korea, Taiwan and Rhodesia—between them spend more than $9-billion a year on defense, which is almost twice as much as Japan, and their spending is mounting rapidly. Even without open or clandestine assistance from Western countries, they already possess the scientific and engineering skills, and the materials and economic resources, to manufacture fairly sophisticated weaponry at reasonable cost.

Sales to and possibly joint production with other countries facing increasing difficulty in procuring arms from the U.S. such as Iran, Turkey, Brazil, Argentina and Chile, which between them spend more than $15-billion a year on defense, would more than double the size of the market. In fact all these countries together represent an arms market almost half the size of European NATO (NATO excluding the U.S., and Canada), and they would not require some

161

of the extremely expensive weaponry that NATO deploys like intercontinental ballistic missiles and nuclear submarines. In addition, if such a group of nations were able to supply advanced armaments at reasonable cost, they would become an attractive alternative supplier to other countries unwilling to become too dependent on America, Soviet or even West European sources, such as Japan, India and Indonesia—these 3 alone spend more than $9-million a year on defense.

The basics already exist for a considerable degree of rationalization and specialization of production of arms and other military equipment among the threatened countries. For instance South Africa would be the logical supplier to the group of war materials such as special steels, explosives, heavier types of armaments such as tanks, and nuclear weapons. Israel would logically concentrate on developing the highly-sophisticated technology that modern weaponry requires, on aircraft and on missiles. Taiwan, with the most advanced shipbuilding industry among the group, could logically become the supplier of naval vessels of all kinds. South Korea could specialize in artillery and small arms. Rhodesia could mass-produce ammunition.

Cooperation could involve, not only joint military production and interchange of intelligence, but also mutual defense pacts. South Africa has already established a precedent in this, having in the past sent fighter squadrons to defend South Korea in the Korean War, Jewish volunteers to fight in Israel's several wars, and paramilitary police to aid Rhodesia in its battle against terrorists.

Collaboration could also extend to pursuit of common political objectives, such as ideological warfare against Communism, and to economic objectives, such as mutual trade and specialization in industrial development. South Africa, Israel, Iran, Turkey, South Korea, Taiwan and Rhodesia together represent a grouping with an economic strength equal to that of Canada, and with a growth rate exceeding that of any existing group of nations. If the major South American countries such as Brazil and Argentina joined in, the resulting alliance would have an economic strength equal to that of West Germany, the world's fourth largest economy.

Rationalization and specialization among this group, as in the case of weapons production, could deliver considerable benefits. For instance, if 5 countries headed by Brazil and South Africa were to coordinate the routing, airplane purchase and servicing aspects of their airlines, they would represent a group carrying one-fifth the domestic and international passenger traffic of all U.S. airlines. In manufacturing, South Africa could concentrate on metals, heavy engineering and inorganic chemicals; Israel on scientific, precision and similar high-technology products; Taiwan on medium engineering, electronics and shipbuilding; South Korea on light engineering, textiles and other consumer products; Iran on supply of oil and petrochemicals; Brazil on metals and automobiles.

All this may seem a pipedream at present. But there is a foundation for such a grouping in the closer relations that are already developing among several of the countries mentioned. The pipedream could become a reality if the U.S. continues to alienate itself from many of its traditional smaller allies, and those allies feel that their survival as independent nations depends on their collaboration with others who share their fear of Communist aggression and subversion. The Carter Administration has already begun to cut down U.S. arms sales, saying that in future arms transfers will only be allowed "as an exceptional foreign policy instrument, to be used only in instances where it can be clearly demonstrated that the transfer contributes to our national security." American determinations of U.S. national security are hardly likely to be regarded by nations such as Israel and Iran as the proper basis for determining their defensive strengths. Nor are such countries likely to rely on alternative suppliers such as France, which has proved as unreliable as the U.S. in the past (Israel and South Africa are examples).

Economic developments could buttress arms supply pressures. If the world's economic troubles worsen, if the post-War "golden age of capitalism" is over and there is a tendency to return to the protectionism of the Thirties, the "pariah states" could be hit hard. They could find themselves restricted in their freedom to sell to major markets like the U.S. and the European Economic Community, while their exports, principally commodities and simpler industrial products, could face a permanent situation of low prices. They could then develop an acute sense of being discriminated against by the advanced nations, driving them into alliance with fellow-sufferers.

Certainly the "Fifth World option" is one that South Africa, which possesses remarkable mineralogical, industrial, scientific and military resources for its size, will consider seriously.

163

19.

Race relations —
what must be done

The situation of increasing international isolation and escalating danger requires from South Africa strong leadership, radical policy changes and energetic preparation. We have to be implacable in our determination, yet fast on our feet. Jimmy Carter may believe that "in the life of the human spirit, words are action," but in the Republic's circumstances an old proverb is more appropriate: "Actions speak louder than words." Our survival will depend on our own actions much more than on what the U.S. or others do to us.

To meet the increasing difficulties that the Republic can expect, we need what the Defense Force called a "total national strategy" in its 1977 report to Parliament, and what the Chief of Army Staff (Operations) General Jack Dutton has described as an "orchestrated" response—military, political, diplomatic, economic, psychological, ideological, cultural and semantic. So far the building of "Fortress South Africa" has largely been confined to developing powerful military forces and establishing strategic stocks of a wide range of essential materials, ranging from oil to bearings, whose supply would be threatened by international sanctions. Defensive preparations have to be extended, rapidly, to many other areas.

The most important of these, without any doubt, is race relations. The Chief of Army Logistics, General G.J.J. Boshoff, has described this as the weak link in the Republic's defenses. "We will never be able to withstand modern threats unless all the nations of South Africa strive for solidarity and form a solid communal front against outside attack," he has said. "Not everyone can pull on a uniform and handle a gun, but everyone can make a contribution to our wellbeing through the enhancement of good and harmonious human and race relations." Humiliating others by word and deed undermined the White nation and amounted to "handing our communal fatherland to the enemy on a plate." While basic cultural differences would probably always exist, many Blacks "are no longer pleased with the traditional social segregation regulations. They revolt against our hardnecked refusal to make new concessions about social intercourse with them."

The concern of the military about race relations is not really surprising, as its leaders have steeped themselves in knowledge of revolutionary war for many years, and are intensely aware that victory in such conflicts is 80 per cent political and only 20 per cent military. What is more encouraging is the increasing recognition of this reality in other quarters. Prime Minister Vorster stressed in a 1977 statement: "My policy and that of my party is *not* based on the belief that one race is superior to another. In the economic and in the social sphere the Government has clearly expressed its intention to do away as fast as possible with restrictive measures which discriminate on the basis of race and color." Information Secretary Rhoodie told Parliament in his department's 1977 annual report that there was a need for "imaginative large-scale moves ... away from racial discrimination." Deputy Information Minister Louis le Grange has revealed that the Cabinet has accepted a still-secret plan to abolish racial discrimination, and that this is being implemented "step by step".

Vorster's "as fast as possible" cannot mean everything, now, at once, given the political, social and economic realities of an ethnically compartmentalized society. Foreign Minister Botha cautioned the U.N.: "There are schools of thought, traditions and practises which cannot be changed overnight." There was also a proviso in the Prime Minister's statement, for he added that discriminatory measures would only be removed "as and when the original rationale for their adoption (viz. to avoid friction and confrontation between the various population groups) falls way."

An example of practical difficulty is the closing of the wide gap between spending on the education of Black and White children. Although allocations for Black education rise sharply every year, much of the additional money is swallowed up providing facilities for additional schoolgoers, as the population of Blacks, Coloreds and Asians is growing much faster than that of Whites. A move to immediate per capita equality is impossible, as it would require a diversion of resources equivalent to a cut of about 25 per cent in the living standards of all races in South Africa.

For several years now there has been a clearly identifiable speeding up of the process of change, and an alteration in the direction of change, in race relations in South Africa. It began with a hard-to-quantify change in the attitudes of White workers towards the upgrading of Black, Colored and Asian workers: for instance 20,000 Blacks were able to take over jobs previously done by Whites on the State-owned railroads, while 5,000 Blacks moved into skilled positions in the Post Office. Then came an active concern among the business community and in the Government with raising sharply the living standards of their Black, Colored and Asian workers: over the 1972-76 period, their average real earnings jumped 36 per cent, while those of White workers grew only 2 per cent. The Government accelerated the rate of growth of its spending on Black education, and began a crash program to upgrade industrial skills of Black workers, with the building of a chain of training centers across the country and introduction of handsome tax benefits for businessmen prepared to spend to train their Black employees.

Here are a few other examples cited by Government spokesmen of progress toward improved race relations:

- Desegregation of public facilities such as many hotels, restaurants, post offices, libraries, parks, theaters and art galleries. Thousands of "Whites only" signs have disappeared from places such as elevators, park benches and beaches.
- Compulsory segregation of sport has been ended, and multiracial meetings are now commonplace. Racially integrated national bodies to represent sportsmen of all races are now viewed with favor, and international representative teams are being picked on a merit basis.
- Although the laws governing segregation at the workplace

have not been repealed, they are falling into disuse and many employers are integrating workplaces gradually.

- Industrial areas previously available only to Whites are being desegregated to allow Colored and Asian businessmen to establish plants there.

- The principle of equal pay for equal work, irrespective of race, has been accepted by the Government, and it has acted in recent years to close the Black/White income gap faster than the private sectors of the economy other than mining. For instance, during 1976, pay increases averaged 11 per cent in real terms for Blacks working for the central Government, provincial administrations and local authorities, compared with —3 per cent for Whites and 1 per cent for Blacks employed in all industries.

- The ruling party has accepted the principle that public expenditure on education of Blacks, Coloreds and Asians should eventually be equal on a per capita basis to spending on White children. Annual Government spending on Black education multiplied six times over the 12 years to 1976, and in the current fiscal year (1977/78) money allocated to Black schools in the White-primacy areas has jumped more than 50 per cent.

- Blacks and Coloreds have been appointed to senior positions in the public service. Blacks have been commissioned as officers in the police and prisons service. Colored officers have been commissioned in the army, and White rank-and-filers are fully subordinate to them. Black, Colored and Asian components of the armed forces are being established and expanded.

- Blacks are to be given full local government powers in their own residential townships in the White-primacy areas, and are being allowed to buy their own homes. In Soweto, for instance, by July 1977 1,200 had already done so and 10,000 applications were being processed.

- The Government has accepted many of the recommendations of a multiracial commission to improve social, economic and political conditions of the 2½-million Coloreds.

- There is a growing political consultation between Whites and other races at all levels, with regular meetings between Black, Colored and Asian leaders and the Cabinet, and representation of Coloreds and Asians on official bodies such as the

Prime Minister's Economic Advisory Council, the Wage Board and the Unemployment Insurance Board.

● The Government is pressing ahead with its plans to give more political authority to Blacks on a decentralized, ethnic group basis. Transkei, a territory 50 per cent larger than Maryland, has already been given complete independence. Another homeland, Bophuthatswana, will become independent December 1977.

● Namibia, administered by South Africa under an old (and disputed) League of Nations mandate, is to be given its independence on a majority-rule basis.

The intensely frustrating thing for many of us who want to see radical change in South Africa's ethnic policies is that such progress is never recognized abroad. It does not suit the country's critics to publicize these developments. In any case, they regard White supremacy as the fundamental issue, and therefore don't see the changes that have been made as relevant. Most people in the U.S. and elsewhere, when acquainted with racial advances, tend to regard them as minimal changes that should have been made long ago.

Well, maybe they should have been. But they are not minimal in the context of the South African environment. They are substantial and they are important in that they set the scene for more fundamental change. The trouble is, lack of recognition abroad that any progress is being made undercuts those within the policymaking group who argue for change partly on the grounds that it will make South Africa more acceptable internationally. If this lack of recognition persists, their influence could weaken.

Many South Africans, and I am among them, argue for change not on the grounds that it will make the Republic more popular internationally (it won't), but for 3 other reasons. Firstly, the Government's policy must evolve more rapidly along the lines of development rather than separation to make it morally defensible. Secondly, South Africa must make its case more presentable and comprehensible to help its many friends in the U.S. and other Western countries. Thirdly, South Africa cannot be defended against the many who threaten it unless the Whites win a large number of Blacks, Coloreds and Asians to their cause and keep most of the rest neutral. They already have a stake in the system. But it needs to be made more obvious. This can be done, as has been proved in a limited way in Rhodesia, where two-thirds of the Government's security forces are Black—and they are loyal and effective, notwithstanding the propaganda war being waged against them by the Black revolutionary movements.

I am not sufficiently qualified to provide a detailed check list of steps that could be taken to improve race relations, but there are some obvious broad areas where action has to be taken—and fast. One is the area of job reservation, which now only affects a very small number of White workers, and which in any case no longer provides them with effective protection against "unfair competition." Another is the odious area of prohibition of interracial sex. Repeal of the anti-miscegenation clause of the Immorality Act and of the Mixed Marriages Act would hardly be likely to lead to widespread miscegenation (it did not occur before these laws were brought in). The small-scale practical, political and social problems that would arise could surely be handled in civilized and sensible ways. The existence of these legal prohibitions is both an insult to human dignity and an offensive symbol internationally of the worst aspects of our ethnic policies. Incidentally, mixed marriages were illegal in 16 U.S. states till as recently as 1967, when the Supreme Court ruled the laws unconstitutional.

A third area is political representation. The Government's policy as it now stands makes inadequate provision for urban Blacks, yet they could be accommodated within the framework of the separate development philosophy. A fourth is the consolidation of the homelands. The homelands concept would be much more acceptable both to Blacks and to foreigners if each homeland did not consist of several scattered pieces of territory but a single contiguous territory. White farmers do not necessarily have to be bought out at great expense to the taxpayer to achieve this—redrawing of boundaries to incorporate White farms in homelands with financial and political guarantees for the farmers encouraged to stay and work for the Black governments as White farmers work in Zambia and Kenya, would achieve the objectives of consolidation without insupportable cost.

A fifth area is continuing administration of Black townships such as Soweto as "White" areas by White officials. The result is the worst of all worlds, because Blacks are given in a paternalistic way considerable material advantages such as clinics, libraries, sports facilities, schools and subsidized houses and transportation, yet denied the freedom to rule themselves, police themselves, tax themselves, determine who shall be allowed to reside and who not, what a businessman may do and what not. The resulting frustration shows itself in the destruction of clinics and libraries as well as beerhalls as "symbols" of White authority and White paternalism. If Blacks owned their own houses and built schools at their own expense, and had the freedom to govern the townships according to their own political ideas and cultural traditions, they would identify themselves with stability rather than revolution, and the young Marxist revolutionaries would suddenly find themselves having a very hard time indeed—from their own people. If the revolutionaries themselves had to shoulder some responsibility for the development of their people, they would become less militant. The Government is already taking action in this sphere. I hope it will be sufficiently far-reaching.

Many aspects of South Africa's ethnic policies do not lend themselves to easy change. For instance, it would hardly benefit either Blacks or Whites to abolish the much-disliked pass laws if this led to the swamping of the Black townships with people for whom there are no jobs, producing again the kind of slums that South Africa has spent so much money and effort to abolish since the War. Nor is it sensible to try to force the integration of schools or residential areas, when this would lead to explosive friction of the kind that the U.S., with its far more advantageous basic situation, has seen and continues to see. Nor can the income gap between Black and White simply be closed by raising Black pay without raising Black productivity to equivalent degree. We have had some of this bleeding-heart do-goodism in recent years, and this has led inevitably to a massive increase in Black unemployment, which helps nobody.

But one does not have to be dogmatically opposed to separate development, one does not have to be a bleeding heart liberal, to recognize that there is not only a great deal wrong with race relations policies and practices, but also a great deal that can be done to improve them, in the long-term interests of Whites as well as Blacks. We have to make those changes because they are right and sensible—not because we need to heed our foreign critics.

20.

Fortress South Africa

South Africa faces the prospect of a confrontation with the U.S.—a confrontation in which the Americans will have the public support of the entire world, and the private backing of most of it. Nobody who grasps the reality of American power, economic and otherwise, and American determination to deploy that power to reach objectives, no-one who knows how dangerously isolated the Republic has become in the world, will under-estimate the danger that such a confrontation poses. Danger not only to the survival of White South Africa as a stable, democratic and civilised nation, free of the loathsome corruption, brutality and incompetence that is so typical of the African environment, but also danger to the progress of Black South Africa toward a more rewarding material, political, emotional and spiritual relationship with White South Africa in the land that both must share.

The collapse of White authority north of the Limpopo and the new militancy of Black opinion have begun polarization on racial lines. The U.S. now seems determined to pursue policies that will strengthen that process of polarization. It is a process leading straight toward the very violence that the U.S. claims to be most afraid of.

Many people in Western countries, including not a few Americans, and even including conservatives who are temperamentally well-disposed toward South Africa, just don't believe that South Africa can "hold out". They have seen the U.S. humbled by North Vietnam. They have seen White communities crumble elsewhere in Africa. "South Africa is doomed," one leading South African was told by a member of the Carter Cabinet. This resignation on the part of those who doubt our capacity to resist is more dangerous than the active position of liberals and Marxists in the U.S. and elsewhere who are convinced that we are evil and seek to destroy us. We have to make it clear that we will "hold out".

South Africa will survive as an independent nation, of that I have no doubt. It has the power, the resources and the determination to ensure that survival. Like Switzerland, it can make the price of its conquest too high for potential aggressors to accept. Like Israel, it knows that it can only lose a war once, and it is prepared to take half the world with it if faced with extinction. Unlike the Whites of Algeria, Angola and Mozambique, South Africa's cannot be betrayed by a metropolitan government grown weary of war and anxious to cut its losses. Unlike Rhodesia, South Africa does not depend on any lifelines of oil or ammunition or whatever—ultimately, like the U.S., it can survive entirely on its own if it is forced to. Its military power is so great in relation to any likely enemy, either conventional or revolutionary, that it could not be contested except by one of the two superpowers. The British strategist Dr. Peter Janke has said that "of all the threatened areas in the world today, South Africa strategically has a unique autonomy of action, is best able to defend herself, and is best able to stand alone if necessary."

South Africa has great resources that it can use simultaneously to ward off the threats of the international community and to transform its society—provided it has the political will. South Africans come from the toughest stock there is: Boers who trekked into the African wilderness, who won the battle of Blood River, who fought the British Empire at the height of its power; Brits who faced the Armada, Napoleon and Hitler, who went through the slaughter of Paaschendael, who stood against the Zulu impis at Rorke's Drift; Huguenots who accepted martyrdom or exile rather than break faith; Hollanders and Germans that even the Roman legions could not conquer. Whatever South Africans' weaknesses, capacity for stubborn, unyielding resistance cannot be one of them. It is inherent in the national character.

After Rhodesia declared its independence in 1965, the almost unanimous opinion of the "experts" was that Ian Smith would not last more than a few weeks. Almost a dozen years later, his independent republic was still struggling bravely on. Is it really credible that South Africa, whose basic strengths are immeasurably greater, will not survive an international offensive as long, or 5 times as long, or 10 times as long ... or until the world is bored with the whole thing, and/or political interests are viewed quite differently?

South Africa has many friends as well as enemies within the U.S.—it is just unfortunate that so few of them are in the White House. It is up to South Africans to help those friends to mobilize political support to block at least the more extreme and potentially dangerous anti-South African measures that are being considered by the Administration, such as American participation in a U.N. "Peace" Force for Southern Africa.

More money is spent each year in America on advertising aspirin than in promoting South Africa. Yet words are far cheaper than bullets and can be just as effective in winning a war, particularly with the U.S. Administration—as the Communist side found in Vietnam. Prime Minister Vorster is reputed to have said that a year of psychological warfare is cheaper than one day of hot war. Certainly an annual budget of $18-million for promotional activities worldwide, including operations within the Republic, looks minute compared with the $350 million spent on commercial advertising in South Africa every year, or compared with a military budget better than $2-billion. South Africa needs to spend much more than it does on psychological warfare, and in particular it needs to spend much more within the U.S.

Americans are particularly sensitive to media leadership, and their political system in turn, being the world's most democratic, is particularly sensitive to public opinion. The media can be influenced. Journalists do not constitute a monolithic bloc of bone-headed prejudice. Even Information Secretary Rhoodie, who has made scathing attacks on the American Press, says that in the U.S. "there are no more than 40 or 50 newspapers out of a total of over 1,700 dailies which present a problem to us." This handful may, as Rhoodie says, be "among the biggest and most influential," but their influence is a lot less than many South Africans believe. The first newspaper a Congressman picks up to read—because its content and comment is the most important to him—is his hometown daily, not the *Washington Post*. This is a section of the

173

American Press used skilfully by other countries with image problems, such as Iran. If South African leaders speak out boldly, they can get far more publicity, for free, than they can ever get from paid advertising—this is something that men like Foreign Minister Botha and Information Minister Mulder understand.

Even papers like the *Washington Post*—which is a pillar of the liberal establishment, especially after its role in the Watergate affair—are becoming more moderate on South Africa. The *Post* has come out in favor of more U.S. investment in the Republic, not less. And it has expressed "grave misgivings" about the Administration's "undeclared psychological warfare" against the Republic.

South Africa's enemies in the U.S. including those within the Administration, are not supermen. They have blundered before and must do so again, as many of the premises on which they are basing their arguments and policies are false (for instance, the conviction that human rights is an issue that appeals to Third World leaders). If they see that their offensive is failing because of South Africa's determined resistance, ultimately the Carter Administration will settle for very much less than one man, one vote. And notwithstanding the indignant denials that are made today, it could settle for a solution within the framework of the separate development concept.

South Africa needs a multi-faceted response to deal with its challenging situation. A part of it, as I have already indicated, is a speeding up of the process of change in all aspects of race relations (social, political and economic). This process of change will strengthen the position of White South Africa in the long run, as there can be no argument that its security ultimately depends on some degree of accommodation of Black, Colored and Asian demands. Another aspect is preparation for economic war, and I shall deal with that later.

A third is ideological preparation. South Africans must be made more aware of the dangers they face, or what they are fighting for—and what they are fighting against. Survival will depend to a considerable degree on morale. As General George C. Marshall said: "You can have all the material in the world, but without morale it is largely ineffective." South Africa's morale will be influenced by how well-prepared the Government is seen to be when the crunch comes, and also by how well-informed South Africans are about what they can expect to face. Nothing is so frightening as the unknown, and a crisis mentally prepared for is a crisis already half overcome. South Africans should not be despondent about their changed situation.

Their strengths are greater than they realize; there are many weaknesses in the forces ranged against them.

A fourth facet is the way that South Africa handles its relations with the outside world, which until "Pik" Botha took over the Foreign Affairs Department was largely an unmitigated disaster, making us the laughing-stock of chancellories around the globe. As lobbyist DeKieffer said in a broadcast over South African radio: "It is hard to respect someone who grovels all the time, and you don't ally yourself with those you don't respect. Till now, South African foreign policy has not reflected the character of the South African people."

It is extremely important that we stop confusing words with actions (ours and the Americans). Our maxim ought to be the one set by Teddy Roosevelt three-fourths of a century ago: "Speak softly and carry a big stick—you will go far." South Africa's policy up till now could fairly be described as one of talking tough and carrying matchsticks.

The most dangerous thing we can do is to believe that by making one concession after another to Western pressure, particularly over Rhodesia and Namibia, that we are "gaining time" for our own strategic preparations. We are not buying time, we are selling it, for the process of making one concession after another has so lowered respect for South Africa worldwide that the West is becoming increasingly optimistic that it will be able to destroy the Republic without undue expense or inconvenience. They are positively encouraged to try sanctions. By making concessions we do not build up moral credit or an inventory of brotherly love in Washington, London or Paris. Carter is no god, and the Western nations are not our loving parents. Other countries look cynically and coldbloodedly to their own interests, as their current governments see them.

This is not just my view. Not just John Chettle's view. It is also the view of a large number of South Africa's friends in the U.S. And it is the view of the Johannesburg *Sunday Times'* Ken Owen, who knows far more about America than I could ever hope to. He wrote in May 1977: "Nothing seems as calculated to fail as the notion that by acceding to small pressures, the big pressures can be avoided. This is the lesson of Munich. Each concession will embolden opponents abroad to try additional pressure, and in the end they will inevitably go beyond our limits of tolerance. The result would be disaster by miscalculation."

We should certainly take no lead in provoking the hostility of the

Western powers, but we must be prepared to penalize them for every hostile measure that they take against us, with a policy of phased response. They must be made to pay for their sins, so they slowly learn that sinning against South Africa does not pay.

For instance it makes no sense to cooperate with the U.S. Administration in pursuing policies to destabilize Rhodesia when the chaos that would undoubtedly result if such policies succeed would polarize White and Black opinion within the Republic and bring terrorist camps to our borders. We should rather collaborate only in bringing about a stable, pro-Western, multiracial administration that serves our national interests as well as Rhodesia's. It makes no sense to tear down a lightning conductor so lightning strikes your house. It would be quite crazy to throw away South Africa's most powerful bargaining counter in the world—its de facto control over almost all chrome deposits—by losing its influence over the critical Rhodesian reserves. It would be almost as foolish to lose effective control over Namibia, with something like one-tenth of the world's uranium reserves.

It makes no sense to suffer economic sanctions without responding with sanctions against those who bully us. If nations refuse to allow further investment in South Africa on political grounds, they should no longer be permitted to enjoy the dividends, interest payments and other real benefits provided by the South African economy. If countries are willing to contemplate restrictions on trade as a political weapon, then they surely cannot expect to continue enjoying unrestricted access to one of the world's great markets. If governments are prepared to use their intelligence and propaganda agencies to destabilize the internal situation in the Republic, then they should be prepared for South Africa to start interfering in their internal affairs. If countries are prepared to harbor and aid those who seek to subvert Southern African governments, then they should not be surprised if South Africa should start heeding appeals for help from Black dissidents seeking to restore democracy in those very countries.

There are many weapons that South Africa could use if it is forced to defend itself. For instance one American well-acquainted with Washington behavior suggests that the Republic could "stop the Administration in its tracks" by developing nuclear weapons and announcing its willingness to sell these to other threatened anti-Communist nations such as South Korea and Taiwan (South Korea has already asked the U.S. for nuclear arms, and has been

176

refused).

If the Cape sea route is as unimportant as many of South Africa's critics suggest, then there could be no objection to the Republic's applying strict anti-pollution and fishing control measures to all vessels passing through its 200-mile territorial waters. If the inspections necessary to enforce these measures resulted in extremely costly shipping delays, for American controlled companies flying Liberian or Panamanian flags, then they would merely be an unfortunate side-effect of legitimate measures to protect South Africa's environment and its economic resources.

If the importance of the Republic's minerals is "exaggerated", then there could be no serious objection to organization of either secret or public cartels to boost substantially the world prices of South Africa's major products. The Russians would probably be delighted to participate, as they have been quite willing to collaborate discreetly with both South Africa and Rhodesia in the past. South Africa has always said that it would not participate in cartels, yet it initiated and still operates the most enduring and successful of all cartels—controlling the marketing of diamonds.

Political leverage is a powerful factor in the U.S. For instance, Senator George McGovern of South Dakota is an ultra-liberal, and ultra-liberals are strongly opposed to farm subsidies. But not McGovern. He's in favor of them, because his political survival in South Dakota depends on it. South Africa has to learn to use its leverage on Congress by applying pressure to sensitive points. For instance, if it threatened to cartelize vital steel alloying minerals like chrome and manganese, this would endanger metals industries jobs in Ohio, Pennsylvania and New York states. If it threatened to boycott U.S. corporations and their products in response to a White House offensive, this would immediately endanger jobs in California, Illinois and Washington states. This is a system that other pariah states, like Israel, Iran, Taiwan and South Korea, understand and employ to considerable advantage.

"You must show more chutzpah," advises one friendly American. "Show strength—but don't challenge the U.S. too directly. Drop garbage phrases like 'Western values' that Americans do not even understand. Start negotiating. At present you just hand out one concession after another, demanding nothing in return. Demand an eye for an eye. Don't back down when you're threatened—just counter-threaten with something just as nasty. Start muttering about hot pursuit operations into Angola and Mozambique, ending cooperation over Namibia, fomenting revolution in Africa. You'll put Washington into a tailspin."

Another sign of South African strength would be possession of nuclear weapons. Some foreign observers, French Prime Minister Raymond Barre among them, have claimed that the Republic already has them. This has repeatedly been denied by the South African Government. If in fact the Republic does have them, it should say so. If it does not, then it should develop them—quickly. It has the scientific and technical resources to do so, and the cost would be moderate. It is true, as some have argued, that nuclear weapons would have limited military value in the kinds of war that we could face. But this overlooks the enormous psychological value and political leverage that their possession would provide. The atom bomb is a symbol of strength—a symbol that India, a poorer and less threatened country, came to regard as a necessity. The world respects strength, and South Africa must have respect if it is to survive. Sir Winston Churchill said, when he announced Britain's decision to develop the atom bomb: "Safety is the sturdy child of terror."

Finally, let's look at the South African economy. This is the area where we seem to be least prepared for a confrontation with the U.S. that could expand into various kinds of worldwide sanctions against South Africa. We depend more heavily on international trade than most other countries, with 28 per cent of national production being sold on foreign markets and 29 per cent of domestic requirements being supplied from abroad. A significant proportion of export sales is made up of items such as gold and fruit that are potentially susceptible to sanctions or punitive measures. Imports largely comprise capital goods (about two-thirds of what the country requires), processed and partially-manufactured goods as inputs for South African plants, crude oil, and sophisticated weaponry.

Due both to misfortune and maladministration, our foreign reserves situation is shocking. On July 1, 1977, they stood at a mere $829-million, or enough for little more than one month's imports. What's more, this figure was bolstered by heavy short-term borrowings. If this were deducted, the country's net reserves were a red-ink figure of about $1½-billion. The Bank for International Settlements has revealed that South Africa has plunged deeply into debt in recent years. Its net borrowing from foreign commercial banks at the end of 1976 stood at $6.2-billion, or almost as much as the Soviet

Union, with $3.4-billion due for repayment or rolling over during 1977.

The paucity of the Republic's "war chest", the excessive dependence on international trade, and the need to stimulate the domestic economy, if only to create jobs for Blacks, all argue for far more radical policy actions than the Government has so far been willing to contemplate. We must over the next few years produce a surplus aggregating something like $10-billion on our balance of payments to pay off short-term debts and build up net reserves equivalent to about six months' imports. We must replace a significant proportion of our imports of capital goods, semi-manufactures, oil and weapons with locally-made alternatives or substitutes. We must stop the pool of Black unemployed growing at something like 1,000 a day.

There are two basic policy approaches toward achieving such dramatic changes. One is to use the market, the other is to use controls. Personally, I would prefer the market, which is more in keeping with the free enterprise system. If we remove both exchange and import controls, the value of the rand in terms of dollars, pounds or marks would plummet as the chickens grabbed their bacon rind and ran. Pretty soon, the rand's value would stabilize at a lower level. At that point, imported goods would look extremely expensive compared with local alternatives or potential alternatives, and imports would decline. Exports would look highly profitable. Cost-push inflationary pressures would look terrifying, but the Government could neutralize inflation entirely by continuing to keep a tough clamp on growth of the money supply.

The trouble is, such a policy requires enormous political courage, and would look far too radical to the Pretoria bureaucrats. Also a market policy provides the Government with no weapons for selective use against various foreign nasties, as, for instance, an import control system does. Therefore the control method looks the more likely, especially as the apparatus to apply it is already established and operational. This must mean tighter control over capital inflows, dividend and interest payments, imports and even exports. We could see cuts in foreign exchange allowances for travellers going abroad, cuts in the amount of capital and current income that emigrants are allowed to take out of the Republic, and cuts in imports of consumer luxuries such as French wine, Polish jam and Chinese toys.

We could see dramatic changes in some aspects of the economy that are quite absurd for a semi-developed country wallowing in recession and threatened with commercial isolation—such as a dozen different automobile plants for a market 3 per cent the size of America's, 3 separate Government departments plus 22 control boards plus a special bank for a single sector of the economy (agriculture) producing less than one-tenth of GNP, and a carefully structured system of tax and labor laws to encourage businessmen to import expensive machinery rather than create jobs for relatively cheap local labor.

Whether market or control methods are used, however, the South African economy faces a period of considerable disruption as it adjusts structurally to totally new circumstances. That disruption is going to hurt a lot of people, but the sooner we face up to it and the more prepared mentally the business community is for it, the easier the transformation will be. It cannot be avoided. Far-reaching adjustments will have to be made in South Africa, just as they were made in Rhodesia, where it was amazing how a handful of industrialists and farmers brought about a high level of self-sufficiency in an economy one-tenth the size of South Africa's. The sooner we start, the more prepared our country will be for whatever the future holds.

South Africa has been a lotus-eaters' land for too long, drifting along without adapting to the dramatic changes in the African environment and in the wide world beyond it. The kinds of economic madness already referred to could only thrive in the environment of extraordinary prosperity that South Africa has experienced since the War. Perhaps because we Whites, who have been running the show, have enjoyed living standards equivalent to those of North America and Western Europe, we have tended to identify with the kinds of economic thinking and development policies favored there, when the approaches of Third World success stories such as Taiwan, South Korea, Singapore, Brazil and Iran might have been far more appropriate.

South Africa has to a regrettable degree remained "colonial" in its thinking and its policies. It has allowed continuation of a dangerous degree of dependence on foreign countries for its prosperity, at the mercy of commodity price movements over which it has little control. It has stayed psychologically dependent on links with "parent" Britain and other Western nations, yearning for the emotional security of adoption by the U.S. in a big brother, little brother, relationship. It has been ponderous and apathetic in tackling its enormous ethnic problems. It is still caught up in the wonder of romantic and in many ways admirable political and other ideals, quite out of touch with Africa's harsh realities (there are for instance many South African Whites who really believe that a paper Bill of Rights would protect their freedoms under a Black Marxist Government).

All this, inevitably, is going to change if the U.S. and other Western countries are going to force South Africa into isolation. It will be a healthy development if we truly start to think and to act like an independent republic. And if it makes all ethnic communities aware that confrontations within the country will solve no more than external confrontation. They have to evolve a common interdependent future in Southern Africa, based on reasonable human standards—and free of domination by neo-imperialists living far away, whatever their language, skin color or political philosophy. The ultimate irony would be if the Carter policy of confrontation makes White South Africa stronger than ever.

South Africans—all South Africans, not just the Government— have multifold responsibilities to change the international political climate, and in particular to influence the United States toward a more positive attitude, by rooting out the evils in their race relations policy, by promoting understanding of the good, by supporting the authorities in a tougher and more realistic approach to defense, foreign relations and economic self-sufficiency, and by making plain by actions (not words) their determination to survive as a free African nation.